The Complete STEAM OVEN COOKBOOK

250+ Healthy, Flavorful, and Effortless Recipes for Your Steam Oven

Frida Welch

© COPYRIGHT 2025 ALL RIGHT RESERVED

TABLE OF CONTENT

INTRODUCTION 7
GETTING STARTED WITH YOUR STEAM OVEN 8
ESSENTIAL TOOLS AND ACCESSORIES 8

1. Mediterranean Quinoa Salad 10
2. Thai Red Curry Shrimp and Vegetables 10
3. Baked Lemon Garlic Tilapia 10
4. Creamy Avocado Chicken Salad 11
5. Greek Chicken Gyros 11
6. Spinach and Mushroom Stuffed Peppers 11
7. Spinach and Ricotta Stuffed Zucchini Boats 12
8. Lemon Garlic Roasted Chicken 12
9. Roasted Sweet Potato and Kale Soup 12
10. Roasted Cauliflower Soup 13
11. Balsamic Roasted Sweet Potatoes 13
12. Thai Curry Shrimp and Vegetables 14
13. Creamy Mushroom Risotto 14
14. Creamy Lemon Garlic Shrimp 14
15. Stuffed Eggplant with Ground Beef 15
16. Spicy Baked Tofu 15
17. Mediterranean Stuffed Tomatoes 15
18. Creamy Mushroom and Spinach Pasta 16
19. Balsamic Glazed Stuffed Bell Peppers 16
20. Roasted Sweet Potatoes and Kale Salad 17
21. Greek Salad with Lemon Vinaigrette 17
22. Greek Quinoa and Chickpea Salad 17
23. Chicken and Broccoli Alfredo 18
24. Sweet Potato & Black Bean Tacos 18
25. Balsamic Roasted Carrots 19
26. Garlic Herb Chicken Wings 19
27. Broccoli and Cheddar Stuffed Chicken 19
28. Lemon Dill Roasted Potatoes 20
29. Greek Quinoa and Feta Salad 20
30. Lemon Dill Chicken Skewers 20
31. Lemon Garlic Herb Shrimp 21
32. Mediterranean Roasted Chickpeas 21
33. Lemon Herb Rice 21
34. Garlic Parmesan Roasted Broccoli 22
35. Baked Teriyaki Tofu 22
36. Lemon Garlic Roasted Mushrooms 22
37. Mediterranean Stuffed Zucchini 23
38. Thai Peanut Chicken 23
39. Greek Chicken and Rice Salad 23
40. Lemon Garlic Roasted Salmon 24
41. Roasted Stuffed Eggplant 24
42. Sweet Potato and Black Bean Salad 24
43. Greek Quinoa and Chickpea Bowl 25
44. Spaghetti with Creamy Mushroom Sauce 25
45. Balsamic Roasted Veggies 26
46. Zucchini Noodles with Pesto 26
47. Thai Coconut Curry Chicken 26
48. Lemon Herb Roasted Chicken and Veggies 27
49. Roasted Vegetable and Quinoa Bowl 27
50. Lemon Garlic Pork Chops 28
51. Lemon Herb Baked Salmon 28
52. Chicken Cacciatore 28
53. Spinach and Goat Cheese Stuffed Chicken 29
54. Spinach and Feta Stuffed Mushrooms 29
55. Roasted Sweet Potatoes with Cilantro 29
56. Thai Peanut Chicken Salad 30
57. Greek Chicken and Rice 30
58. Creamy Avocado and Spinach Pasta 31
59. Roasted Cauliflower Rice 31
60. Spicy Roasted Sweet Potatoes 31
61. Herb-Crusted Salmon 32
62. Sweet Potato Fries 32

#	Title	Page
63.	Mediterranean Baked Fish	33
64.	Creamy Lemon Chicken Pasta	33
65.	Teriyaki Glazed Tofu	33
66.	Lemon Herb Stuffed Chicken	34
67.	Black Bean and Corn Salad	34
68.	Lemon Rosemary Chicken	34
69.	Balsamic Roasted Stuffed Peppers	35
70.	Thai Red Curry Chicken Soup	35
71.	Lemon Herb Salmon	35
72.	Roasted Garlic Mashed Potatoes	36
73.	Lemon Herb Baked Tilapia	36
74.	Thai Coconut Shrimp	36
75.	Garlic Butter Roasted Carrots	37
76.	Lemon Garlic Shrimp and Vegetables	37
77.	Lemon Herb Roasted Veggies	37
78.	Spinach and Ricotta Stuffed Bell Peppers	38
79.	Moroccan Chicken Tagine	38
80.	Spinach & Feta Stuffed Chicken Breasts	39
81.	Roasted Vegetable Lasagna	39
82.	Stuffed Zucchini with Sausage	40
83.	Spinach and Ricotta Stuffed Eggplant	40
84.	Thai Red Curry Chicken and Vegetables	40
85.	Spinach and Feta Stuffed Chicken	41
86.	Spinach Artichoke Stuffed Chicken	41
87.	Lemon Garlic Herb Roasted Carrots	41
88.	Thai Peanut Chicken Skewers	42
89.	Roasted Cauliflower with Garlic and Herbs	42
90.	Thai Green Curry Vegetables	43
91.	Apple Cinnamon Pork Chops	43
92.	Thai Peanut Chicken Stir-Fry	43
93.	Spaghetti Carbonara	44
94.	Roasted Cauliflower Steaks	44
95.	Lemon Herb Stuffed Mushrooms	44
96.	Sweet Potato and Black Bean Chili	45
97.	Asian-Style Salmon	45
98.	Greek Stuffed Zucchini Boats	45
99.	Mediterranean Roasted Chicken	46
100.	Creamy Avocado Chicken Pasta	46
101.	Creamy Spinach and Ricotta Stuffed Shells	46
102.	Mediterranean Chickpea and Vegetable Salad	47
103.	Roasted Stuffed Bell Peppers	47
104.	Lemon Garlic Roasted Veggies	48
105.	Thai Basil Chicken Stir-Fry	48
106.	Thai Chicken Skewers	48
107.	Greek Lemon Chicken Soup (Avgolemono)	49
108.	Spicy Garlic Shrimp	49
109.	Creamy Tomato Basil Chicken	49
110.	Spinach and Feta Stuffed Peppers	50
111.	Mediterranean Chicken Bake	50
112.	Teriyaki Glazed Carrots	51
113.	Sesame Ginger Pork	51
114.	Garlic Parmesan Roasted Chicken	51
115.	Lemon Garlic Tilapia	52
116.	Tomato Basil Soup	52
117.	Greek Meatballs	52
118.	Balsamic Glazed Roasted Chickpeas	53
119.	Thai Coconut Chicken Soup	53
120.	Pesto Stuffed Bell Peppers	53
121.	Creamy Avocado and Lemon Pasta	54
122.	Greek Stuffed Peppers	54
123.	Balsamic Glazed Carrots	54
124.	Thai Basil Chicken and Vegetables	55
125.	Baked Sweet Potato and Kale Salad	55
126.	Sweet Potato and Chickpea Stew	55
127.	Balsamic Roasted Vegetables	56
128.	Thai Green Curry Chicken	56
129.	Creamy Spinach and Lemon Pasta	57
130.	Mediterranean Quinoa and Chickpea Salad	57
131.	Spinach and Feta Stuffed Zucchini	57
132.	Thai Curry Cauliflower	58
133.	Balsamic Roasted Chicken Thighs	58
134.	Balsamic Glazed Brussels Sprouts	58
135.	Roasted Sweet Potatoes with Maple Syrup	59
136.	Lemon Dill Cod	59

#	Recipe	Page
137.	Spaghetti Squash with Marinara Sauce	59
138.	Garlic Butter Shrimp Scampi	60
139.	Spinach and Ricotta Stuffed Shells	60
140.	Garlic Herb Roasted Turkey Breast	60
141.	Lemon Basil Pasta	61
142.	Spaghetti with Roasted Tomato Sauce	61
143.	Spinach and Mushroom Stuffed Mushrooms	62
144.	Roasted Veggie and Quinoa Salad	62
145.	Balsamic Roasted Cauliflower	62
146.	Chicken Parmesan	63
147.	Curried Cauliflower	63
148.	Creamy Tomato Basil Pasta	63
149.	Thai Basil Chicken	64
150.	Sweet and Spicy Roasted Nuts	64
151.	Greek Quinoa Salad	64
152.	Roasted Beet Salad	65
153.	Greek Stuffed Portobello Mushrooms	65
154.	Roasted Garlic Brussels Sprouts	66
155.	Roasted Stuffed Mushrooms	66
156.	Creamy Lemon Herb Pasta	66
157.	Thai Green Curry Shrimp	67
158.	Caprese Stuffed Chicken	67
159.	Sweet Potato and Black Bean Enchiladas	67
160.	Ginger-Sesame Chicken	68
161.	Roasted Stuffed Acorn Squash	68
162.	Butternut Squash Risotto	69
163.	Herb-Crusted Beef Tenderloin	69
164.	Mediterranean Baked Chicken	69
165.	Greek Lemon Herb Chicken	70
166.	Moroccan Spiced Chickpeas	70
167.	Mediterranean Quinoa and Vegetable Salad	71
168.	Roasted Sweet Potato and Black Bean Chili	71
169.	Creamy Spinach and Artichoke Dip	72
170.	Balsamic Glazed Chicken and Veggies	72
171.	Creamy Lemon Garlic Pasta	72
172.	Creamy Avocado Pasta	73
173.	Balsamic Glazed Roasted Potatoes	73
174.	Balsamic Chicken and Vegetables	73
175.	Balsamic Roasted Brussels Sprouts with Bacon	74
176.	Lemon Herb Roasted Potatoes	74
177.	Lemon Garlic Herb Chicken Thighs	74
178.	Teriyaki Chicken Thighs	75
179.	Greek Stuffed Eggplant	75
180.	Quinoa-Stuffed Zucchini Boats	76
181.	Sweet and Spicy Chicken Stir-Fry	76
182.	Thai Red Curry Beef	77
183.	Lemon Garlic Chicken Thighs	77
184.	Mediterranean Stuffed Peppers	77
185.	Creamy Avocado Chicken and Veggies	78
186.	Thai Spiced Pork Tenderloin	78
187.	Honey Glazed Salmon	79
188.	Garlic Butter Chicken Thighs	79
189.	Greek Chicken and Couscous Salad	79
190.	Chicken and Vegetable Kabobs	80
191.	Roasted Vegetable Medley	80
192.	Honey Mustard Brussels Sprouts	80
193.	Thai Spiced Roasted Chicken	81
194.	Pesto Chicken and Vegetables	81
195.	Roasted Garlic Mashed Cauliflower	81
196.	Lemon Garlic Brussels Sprouts	82
197.	Roasted Red Pepper Hummus	82
198.	Greek Chicken and Quinoa Bowl	82
199.	Honey Soy Glazed Pork	83
200.	Roasted Cauliflower and Chickpea Salad	83
201.	Sweet and Spicy Salmon	84
202.	Baked Honey Mustard Chicken	84
203.	Lemon Herb Roasted Brussels Sprouts	84
204.	Balsamic Glazed Chicken	85
205.	Garlic Butter Mushrooms	85
206.	Creamy Tomato Basil Soup	85
207.	Thai Coconut Chicken and Vegetable Curry	86
208.	Herb-crusted pork Tenderloin	86
209.	Spinach and Ricotta Stuffed Chicken	86
210.	Lemon Butter Roasted Salmon	87

211. Stuffed Portobello Mushrooms ... 87
212. Mediterranean Chickpea Salad ... 87
213. Honey Glazed Carrots ... 88
214. Thai Peanut Shrimp ... 88
215. Pesto Baked Chicken ... 88
216. Cilantro Lime Rice ... 89
217. Spaghetti Squash with Garlic Sauce ... 89
218. Roasted Brussels Sprouts with Bacon ... 89
219. Baked Ziti with Meatballs ... 89
220. Roasted Chicken and Vegetables ... 90
221. Beef Stroganoff ... 90
222. Creamy Pesto Pasta ... 91
223. Garlic Parmesan Asparagus ... 91
224. Cajun Shrimp and Grits ... 91
225. Mediterranean Stuffed Eggplant ... 92
226. Garlic Parmesan Shrimp ... 92
227. Stuffed Bell Peppers ... 92
228. Coconut Curry Shrimp ... 93
229. Lemon Thyme Chicken Thighs ... 93
230. Honey Glazed Brussels Sprouts ... 94
231. Thai Basil Beef Stir-Fry ... 94
232. Chicken Fajitas ... 94
233. Roasted Tomato and Basil Soup ... 95
234. Lemon Garlic Chicken Skewers ... 95
235. Spicy Roasted Chickpeas ... 95
236. Lemon Herb Roasted Chicken Thighs ... 96
237. Creamy Broccoli Soup ... 96
238. Roasted Sweet Potatoes with Cilantro Lime ... 96
239. Sweet and Sour Pork ... 97
240. Roasted Cauliflower and Spinach Salad ... 97
241. Mediterranean Chickpea and Feta Salad ... 97
242. Roasted Sweet Potato and Kale Salad ... 98
243. Lemon Dill Roasted Vegetables ... 98
244. Spinach and Artichoke Stuffed Chicken ... 98
245. Garlic Herb Roasted Potatoes ... 99
246. Mediterranean Stuffed Mushrooms ... 99
247. Mediterranean Roasted Vegetables ... 100
248. Stuffed Acorn Squash ... 100
249. Creamy Garlic Parmesan Pasta ... 100
250. Baked Apple Cinnamon Oatmeal ... 101
251. Honey Mustard Glazed Chicken ... 101
252. Maple Glazed Carrots ... 101
253. Lemon Herb Baked Chicken Wings ... 102
254. Thai Red Curry Chicken ... 102
255. Beef and Vegetable Stir-Fry ... 102
256. Thai Basil Beef and Vegetables ... 103
257. Greek Chicken Souvlaki ... 103
258. Tomato and Mozzarella Salad ... 104
259. Shrimp and Asparagus Stir-Fry ... 104
260. Balsamic Roasted Mushrooms ... 104
261. Lemon Thyme Roasted Chicken ... 104
262. Lemon Garlic Chicken and Vegetables ... 105
263. Thai Red Curry Vegetables ... 105
264. Mediterranean Chicken Skewers ... 105
265. Greek Stuffed Tomatoes ... 106
266. Balsamic Roasted Garlic Brussels Sprouts ... 106
267. Balsamic Chicken Thighs ... 106
268. Spiced Lamb Chops ... 107
269. Lemon Garlic Shrimp Pasta ... 107
270. Maple Mustard Chicken ... 108

THE END ... 109

INTRODUCTION

Greetings from The Complete Steam Oven Cookbook, your go-to resource for learning how to cook in a steam oven. Regardless of your level of experience, this cookbook will expand your culinary horizons and improve the taste and consistency of your meals. Steam ovens are a breakthrough method of cooking that preserves essential nutrients, moisture, and color while bringing out the inherent essence of food. They are not simply a fad.

Modern steam ovens elevate the centuries-old practice of using steam as a gentle and efficient cooking method to the forefront of modern kitchens. You can bake, roast, grill, steam, and even reheat meals with ease thanks to these ovens' great versatility. The main advantage of steam cooking is that it keeps food soft and moist without using a lot of butter or oil. This makes it perfect for a wide range of foods, including breads that need exact moisture management, robust meats, and delicate fish fillets.

This book will provide you with a range of recipes designed especially for steam ovens, as well as advice on how to make the most of your device. Every recipe, from simple meals to decadent sweets, will show you how to make the most of the steam oven and make your food come to life in ways that are just not possible with conventional cooking techniques.

In order to improve your food, we've also included useful advice on how to set up your steam oven, how to steam various ingredients, and how to use steam in conjunction with other cooking methods. The steam oven is a vital appliance in every kitchen, whether you want to cook healthier meals, wow visitors with exquisitely prepared food, or just make cooking easier.

GETTING STARTED WITH YOUR STEAM OVEN

It's crucial to comprehend the fundamentals of how your steam oven works before beginning any recipes. There are several varieties of steam ovens, such as:

- **Pure Steam Ovens**: These produce steam, which cooks food gently and evenly, making it perfect for delicate meals, shellfish, and vegetables.
- **Combination Steam Ovens**: These ovens enable roasting, baking, and crisping while retaining moisture by combining steam and convection heat.

❖ **Understanding Steam Oven Cooking Modes**

Different brands and models offer various cooking modes, but common functions include:

- **Steam Mode:** It uses 100% steam and is great for gentle cooking, reheating, and sous vide.
- **Combination Mode:** Mixes steam with dry heat to roast meats, bake bread and create crispy textures.
- **Convection Mode:** Works like a traditional oven with dry heat, ideal for browning and crisping.
- **Sous Vide Mode:** Precise temperature control allows for restaurant-quality sous vide cooking without a water bath.
- **Reheat & Refresh:** Uses steam to gently warm leftovers without drying them out.

❖ **Benefits of Steam Oven Cooking**

- **Healthier Meals**: Retains more vitamins and minerals compared to boiling or frying.
- **Better Texture and Flavor**: Food stays moist and tender while preserving its natural taste.
- **Efficiency**: Cooks faster than traditional ovens, saving time and energy.
- **Versatility**: Can be used for steaming, roasting, baking, reheating, and even sterilizing.

ESSENTIAL TOOLS AND ACCESSORIES

To get the most out of your steam oven, having the right tools and accessories is key. Here are some must-have items:

❖ **Steam-Friendly Cookware**

- **Stainless Steel or Glass Baking Dishes**: Ideal for steaming and roasting.

- **Perforated Steam Trays**: Allow steam to circulate evenly around food for perfect cooking results.
- **Silicone Steam Pans and Mats**: Nonstick and heat-resistant, great for delicate foods like fish or dumplings.

❖ **Temperature and Cooking Aids**

- **Meat Thermometer**: Ensures precision when cooking meats and fish.
- **Oven-Safe Thermometer Probes**: Essential for sous vide and slow-cooked meals.
- **Steam Oven-Safe Parchment Paper**: Helps prevent sticking when baking or steaming.

❖ **Baking and Bread-Making Essentials**

- **Pizza Stone or Baking Steel**: Retains heat for crispier crusts when using combination steam.
- **Proofing Baskets**: Helps create artisan-quality bread with the perfect rise.
- **Spray Bottle for Water Mist**: Useful for adding extra steam when baking crusty loaves.

❖ **Other Useful Accessories**

- **Reusable Silicone Covers**: Use less plastic wrap when proving or heating dough.
- **Oven Gloves and Silicone Grips**: Protect hands from hot steam and trays.
- **Cleaning Cloths and Descaling Agents**: Essential for maintaining your oven's performance.

1. Mediterranean Quinoa Salad

Total Time: 25 minutes | Prep Time: 10 minutes

Ingredients:

1 cup quinoa, rinsed	2 cups water
1 cup cherry tomatoes, halved	1/2 cup cucumber, diced
1/4 cup red onion, finely chopped	1/4 cup kalamata olives, sliced
1/4 cup feta cheese, crumbled	2 tbsp olive oil
1 tbsp lemon juice	1 tsp dried oregano
Salt and pepper to taste	

Directions:

(1) Prepare a steam-safe dish and pour in the water and quinoa. For 15 minutes, or until the quinoa reaches a tenderness, cook it in the steam oven at 210°F (100°C). (2) Allow the quinoa to cool for five minutes. (3) Make a salad by mixing together feta cheese, cucumber, tomatoes, red onion, & olives in a big basin. (4) Toss in the cooked quinoa together with the olive oil, lemon juice, oregano, and salt, in addition to pepper. Incorporate by tossing. (5) Feel free to serve it warm or cool.

2. Thai Red Curry Shrimp and Vegetables

Total Time: 30 minutes | Prep Time: 10 minutes

Ingredients:

1 lb shrimp, peeled and deveined	1 red bell pepper, sliced
1 zucchini, sliced	1 cup snap peas
1 can (14 oz) coconut milk	2 tbsp Thai red curry paste
1 tbsp fish sauce	1 tsp brown sugar
1 tbsp lime juice	Fresh cilantro for garnish

Directions:

(1) Combine salmon sauce, lime juice, red curry paste, brown sugar, and coconut milk in a heatproof bowl. (2) Combine the shrimp and veggies, then toss to combine. (3) After 20 minutes of steaming at 212°F (100°C), the shrimp should be pink, and the veggies should be soft. (4) Serve over steaming rice and top with cilantro.

3. Baked Lemon Garlic Tilapia

Total Time: 20 minutes | Prep Time: 5 minutes

Ingredients:

4 tilapia fillets	2 tbsp olive oil
2 tbsp lemon juice	2 cloves garlic, minced
1 tsp dried oregano	1/2 tsp paprika
Salt and pepper to taste	Lemon slices, for garnish

Directions:

(1) A steam oven preheated to 50% steam may reach temperatures of 190°C (375°F). (2) Coat the olive oil, garlic, lemon juice, oregano, paprika, salt, and pepper in a bowl. Whisk in the olives. (3) Marinate the tilapia fillets in the marinade & place them on a steam-cookable platter. Flake the fish easily with a fork after 12 to 15 minutes in the oven. (4) Steamed veggies should accompany the dish, and lemon slices should be garnished.

4. Creamy Avocado Chicken Salad

Total Time: 20 minutes | Prep Time: 10 minutes

Ingredients:

- 2 boneless, skinless chicken breasts
- 1/4 cup Greek yogurt
- 1/4 tsp garlic powder
- 1/4 cup cherry tomatoes, halved
- 1 tbsp chopped cilantro
- 1 ripe avocado
- 1 tbsp lemon juice
- Salt and pepper to taste
- 1/4 cup red onion, diced

Directions:

(1) After 15 minutes of steaming at 212°F (100°C), the chicken should be well done. Drain and chop. (2) Blend together the mashed avocado, Greek yogurt, lemon juice, garlic powder, salt, & pepper in a bowl. Serve immediately. (3) You may garnish it with chopped cilantro, red onion, cherry tomatoes, and shredded chicken. Mix thoroughly. (4) Put it on salads, lettuce wraps, or sandwiches.

5. Greek Chicken Gyros

Total Time: 40 minutes | Prep Time: 15 minutes

Ingredients:

- 2 boneless, skinless chicken breasts, sliced
- 1 tsp dried oregano
- 1/2 tsp smoked paprika
- 4 pita breads
- 1 tbsp olive oil
- 1 tsp garlic powder
- Salt and pepper to taste
- 1/2 cup tzatziki sauce
- 1/2 cup cherry tomatoes, halved
- 1/4 cup cucumber, sliced
- 1/4 cup red onion, thinly sliced
- Feta cheese, for garnish

Directions:

(1) Lightly coat the chicken in olive oil, then sprinkle with oregano, garlic powder, paprika, salt, and pepper. (2) After placing in a steam-safe dish, cook for 25 minutes at 212°F (100°C) or until done. (3) Use a steam oven to warm pita bread for three minutes. (4) Put together the gyros by dousing each pita with tzatziki sauce, then topping with chicken, tomatoes, onion, and cucumber. (5) Before serving, top with feta cheese.

6. Spinach and Mushroom Stuffed Peppers

Total Time: 35 minutes | Prep Time: 15 minutes

Ingredients:

- 4 large bell peppers (red, yellow, or green), halved and seeds removed
- 1 small onion, finely chopped
- 1 cup mushrooms, finely chopped
- 1 cup cooked quinoa or brown rice
- ½ teaspoon black pepper
- ½ teaspoon red pepper flakes (optional)
- 1 tablespoon olive oil
- 2 cloves garlic, minced
- 2 cups fresh spinach, chopped
- ½ teaspoon salt
- ½ teaspoon dried oregano
- ½ cup shredded mozzarella cheese

Directions:

(1) Set your steam oven to combination (steam and convection) mode and heat it to 375°F, or 190°C. (2) The olive oil should be warmed in a pot over medium heat. Saute the garlic & onion until they are tender. (3) Keep cooking until the mushrooms are soft. Cook the chopped spinach until it wilts, then stir in. (4) Take off the stove and combine the quinoa with the seasonings: pepper, salt, oregano, and red pepper flakes. (5) Spoon half of the mixture into each pepper and sprinkle with mozzarella cheese. (6) Twenty minutes in a steam oven should be enough time to soften the peppers & melt the cheese. (7) Keep heated before serving.

7. Spinach and Ricotta Stuffed Zucchini Boats

Total Time: 30 minutes | Prep Time: 10 minutes

Ingredients:

4 medium zucchini, halved lengthwise	1 tablespoon olive oil
2 cloves garlic, minced	2 cups fresh spinach, chopped
1 cup ricotta cheese	¼ cup grated Parmesan cheese
½ teaspoon salt	½ teaspoon black pepper
½ teaspoon dried basil	½ teaspoon red pepper flakes (optional)
½ cup shredded mozzarella cheese	

Directions:

(1) Put the steam oven on combined heat and bring it up to 375°F, or 190°C. (2) Leave a ¼-inch shell after scooping out the zucchini flesh. Before setting aside, mince the meat. (3) In a skillet, heat the olive oil. Toss in the zucchini and spinach after sautéing the garlic. Simmer until tender. (4) Take it off the fire and combine it with the Parmesan, ricotta, basil, salt, pepper, and red pepper flakes. (5) Spoon the filling into the zucchini halves and sprinkle with mozzarella. (6) Cook in a steam oven for 20 minutes or until the vegetables are soft and the cheese has browned. (7) Keep heated before serving.

8. Lemon Garlic Roasted Chicken

Total Time: 50 minutes | Prep Time: 10 minutes

Ingredients:

1 whole chicken (about 3-4 lbs)	2 tablespoons olive oil
1 lemon, sliced	4 cloves garlic, minced
1 teaspoon salt	½ teaspoon black pepper
1 teaspoon dried thyme	1 teaspoon smoked paprika
½ teaspoon garlic powder	½ teaspoon onion powder

Directions:

(1) In combination mode, bring the steam oven up to 400°F or 200°C. (2) After removing excess moisture, coat the chicken with olive oil. (3) Garlic powder, onion powder, paprika, thyme, and salt are some of the seasonings to consider. (4) Put half of the minced garlic and slices of lemon into the cavity. (5) Roast, basting periodically, for 40 minutes after placing on a roasting pan. (6) Wait five minutes before slicing. Keep heated before serving.

9. Roasted Sweet Potato and Kale Soup

Total Time: 40 minutes | Prep Time: 15 minutes

Ingredients:

- 2 large sweet potatoes, peeled and diced
- 1 small onion, chopped
- 4 cups vegetable broth
- ½ teaspoon black pepper
- ½ teaspoon smoked paprika
- ½ cup coconut milk (optional for creaminess)
- 1 tablespoon olive oil
- 2 cloves garlic, minced
- 1 teaspoon salt
- ½ teaspoon ground cumin
- 2 cups fresh kale, chopped

Directions:

(1) Put the steam oven on combined heat and bring it up to 375°F, or 190°C. (2) Sprinkle salt and pepper over sweet potatoes and toss with olive oil. Cook, covered, for twenty minutes or until soft. (3) Soften the garlic and onion by sautéing them in a saucepan. Gather the roasted sweet potatoes, cumin, paprika, and broth. (4) After 10 minutes of simmering, puree the mixture. (5) Add the chopped kale and cook for five more minutes, stirring occasionally. Coconut milk may be used if preferred. (6) Keep heated before serving.

10. Roasted Cauliflower Soup

Total Time: 35 minutes | Prep Time: 10 minutes

Ingredients:

- 1 medium head cauliflower, chopped
- 1 small onion, chopped
- 1 tablespoon olive oil
- 2 cloves garlic, minced
- 4 cups vegetable broth
- ½ teaspoon black pepper
- ½ teaspoon smoked paprika
- 1 teaspoon salt
- ½ teaspoon ground cumin

*For a dairy-free alternative, you may use half a cup of coconut milk instead of heavy cream.

Directions:

(1) Put the steam oven on combined heat and bring it up to 375°F, or 190°C. (2) Drizzle olive oil, salt, & pepper over the cauliflower. After 20 minutes, roast. (3) Make a sauté pan with the onion and garlic. Sauté the paprika, cumin, roasted cauliflower, and broth. (4) After 10 minutes of simmering, puree the mixture. (5) After 2 minutes of stirring, add coconut milk or heavy cream to the saucepan. (6) Keep heated before serving.

11. Balsamic Roasted Sweet Potatoes

Total Time: 35 minutes | Prep Time: 10 minutes

Ingredients:

- 2 large sweet potatoes, peeled and diced
- 1 tbsp olive oil
- ½ tsp salt
- 1 tsp fresh thyme leaves
- 2 tbsp balsamic vinegar
- 1 tsp honey
- ½ tsp black pepper

Directions:

(1) Bring the steam oven up to temperature on the steam-roast combo setting, which is 400°F or 200°C. (2) After peeling the sweet potatoes, combine them with the olive oil, balsamic vinegar, honey, salt, and pepper in a big basin.

(3) Arrange the potatoes flat on a steam oven pan. (4) Bake for twenty-five minutes, tossing the pan halfway through. (5) Just before serving, top with some fresh thyme.

12. Thai Curry Shrimp and Vegetables

Total Time: 25 minutes | Prep Time: 10 minutes

Ingredients:

1 lb shrimp, peeled and deveined	1 red bell pepper, sliced
1 zucchini, sliced	1 cup coconut milk
2 tbsp red curry paste	1 tbsp fish sauce
1 tsp lime zest	1 tbsp lime juice
1 tbsp fresh cilantro, chopped	

Directions:

(1) Turn the steam oven on to a preheated temperature of 375°F, or 190°C. (2) The red curry paste, fish sauce, lime zest, and lime juice should be whisked with the coconut milk in a dish that can withstand steam. (3) Toss in the zucchini, bell pepper, and shrimp and mix to combine. (4) The shrimp should be cooked for at least 15 minutes in the steamer. (5) Before serving, top with chopped fresh cilantro.

13. Creamy Mushroom Risotto

Total Time: 35 minutes | Prep Time: 10 minutes

Ingredients:

1 ½ cups Arborio rice	3 cups chicken or vegetable broth
1 cup mushrooms, sliced	½ cup grated Parmesan cheese
½ cup heavy cream	1 small onion, diced
2 tbsp butter	1 clove garlic, minced
½ tsp salt	½ tsp black pepper

Directions:

(1) On steam mode, bring the steam oven up to 212°F, or 100°C. (2) In a pot that can withstand steam, mix together the rice, broth, mushrooms, onion, and garlic. (3) Stir occasionally while steaming for 25 minutes. (4) Blend in the heavy cream, Parmesan, and butter. Finish with a pinch of pepper & salt. (5) Allow to cool for five minutes before consumption.

14. Creamy Lemon Garlic Shrimp

Total Time: 20 minutes | Prep Time: 10 minutes

Ingredients:

1 lb shrimp, peeled and deveined	3 cloves garlic, minced
½ cup heavy cream	¼ cup chicken broth
1 tbsp butter	1 tbsp lemon juice
1 tsp lemon zest	½ tsp salt
½ tsp black pepper	1 tbsp fresh parsley, chopped

Directions:

(1) Turn the steam oven on to a preheated temperature of 375°F, or 190°C. (2) Add the shrimp, garlic, heavy cream, chicken stock, butter, lemon juice, zest, salt, and pepper to a dish that can be steam-safe. (3) The shrimp should be cooked thoroughly after 12 to 15 minutes of steaming. (4) Garnish each serving with a little fresh parsley.

15. Stuffed Eggplant with Ground Beef

Total Time: 40 minutes | Prep Time: 15 minutes

Ingredients:

- 2 medium eggplants, halved and hollowed
- ½ lb ground beef
- ½ cup diced tomatoes
- ¼ cup onion, chopped
- 2 cloves garlic, minced
- 1 tbsp olive oil
- ½ tsp salt
- ½ tsp black pepper
- ½ tsp ground cumin
- ¼ cup shredded mozzarella cheese

Directions:

(1) Put the steam oven on combined steam-roast mode and heat it up to 375°F, or 190°C. (2) While the olive oil is heating, sauté the garlic & onion until they release their aroma. (3) Include cumin, ground meat, salt, and pepper. Begin browning the meat. Add the diced tomatoes and stir. (4) Place the eggplant halves in a steam-proof baking dish after stuffing them with the meat mixture. After 25 minutes of steaming, top with mozzarella and continue steaming for five more minutes. (5) Heat and serve immediately.

16. Spicy Baked Tofu

Total Time: 35 minutes | Prep Time: 10 minutes

Ingredients:

- 1 (14-ounce) block of firm tofu, drained & pressed
- 2 tablespoons soy sauce
- 1 tablespoon sriracha sauce
- 1 tablespoon sesame oil
- 1 teaspoon garlic powder
- 1 teaspoon smoked paprika
- ½ teaspoon black pepper
- 1 teaspoon cornstarch

Directions:

(1) Start the steam oven on the combined steam-baking setting and heat it up to 375°F, or 190°C. (2) After chopping the tofu into cubes, use a paper towel to wipe them dry. (3) Whisk together the sesame oil, soy sauce, paprika, garlic powder, & black pepper in a bowl. Add the sriracha and combine well. (4) Marinate the tofu cubes for 5 minutes after tossing them in the sauce. (5) Toss the tofu one more to coat it evenly with cornstarch. (6) Spread the tofu cubes out evenly on a parchment-lined baking sheet. (7) Turn halfway through baking time (20-25 minutes) or until golden brown and slightly crunchy. (8) While still warm, top with a dipping sauce and serve over rice and veggies.

17. Mediterranean Stuffed Tomatoes

Total Time: 40 minutes | Prep Time: 15 minutes

Ingredients:

- 6 large ripe tomatoes
- ½ cup cooked quinoa
- ¼ cup crumbled feta cheese
- ¼ cup chopped kalamata olives
- 2 tablespoons chopped fresh basil
- 1 tablespoon olive oil
- 1 teaspoon dried oregano
- ½ teaspoon salt
- ½ teaspoon black pepper
- 1 garlic clove, minced

Directions:

(1) Set the steam oven to 350°F (175°C) before cooking. (2) To remove the pulp from tomatoes, cut off the tops. Hold on to the pulp. (3) Combine the quinoa, feta, olives, basil, olive oil, oregano, salt, pepper, & garlic in a bowl. (4) Add the chopped tomato pulp to the stuffing after setting aside the pulp. (5) Fill a shallow baking dish with the mixture and stuff each tomato. (6) To make tomatoes that are soft but not mushy, steam-bake for twenty to twenty-five minutes. (7) Warm and serve as an accompaniment or small supper.

18. Creamy Mushroom and Spinach Pasta

Total Time: 30 minutes | Prep Time: 10 minutes

Ingredients:

8 ounces whole wheat pasta	1 tablespoon olive oil
1 small onion, chopped	2 garlic cloves, minced
8 ounces cremini mushrooms, sliced	2 cups baby spinach
1 cup heavy cream or coconut cream	½ cup grated Parmesan cheese
½ teaspoon salt	½ teaspoon black pepper
½ teaspoon nutmeg (optional)	

Directions:

(1) Get the water reservoir of the steam oven full and turn it on to steam mode at 212°F, or 100°C. (2) Pasta cooked al dente requires 8 to 10 minutes in a steamer with holes cut into it. As a side note, in a skillet over medium heat, warm the olive oil. Sauté the garlic and onion for 2 minutes. (3) After 5 minutes, add the mushrooms and simmer until they are tender. (4) Cook the spinach until it wilts, then stir in. (5) Add the nutmeg, salt, pepper, Parmesan, and cream while reducing heat. Thicken by simmering for three to five minutes. (6) Mix in the pasta water, stir it well, and plate it hot.

19. Balsamic Glazed Stuffed Bell Peppers

Total Time: 45 minutes | Prep Time: 15 minutes

Ingredients:

4 large bell peppers (red, yellow, or green)	1 cup cooked brown rice
½ pound ground turkey or plant-based alternative	1 small onion, diced
2 garlic cloves, minced	1 teaspoon dried Italian seasoning
½ teaspoon salt	½ teaspoon black pepper
½ cup tomato sauce	¼ cup balsamic vinegar
1 tablespoon honey	½ cup shredded mozzarella cheese

Directions:

(1) Turn the steam oven's combined steam-baking setting to 375°F, which is 190°C. (2) After you remove the seeds from the bell peppers, cut off the tops. (3) Brown the ground turkey in a skillet with the onion and garlic. Cook for about five minutes over medium heat. (4) Add the tomato sauce, rice, salt, pepper, and Italian seasoning. Stir to combine. Get it out of the oven. (5) Put the peppers on a baking tray after stuffing them with the mixture. (6) Before drizzling the peppers with the mixture, combine the balsamic vinegar & honey in a small basin. (7) Cook, covered, in a steam oven for half an hour. (8) Melt the mozzarella by topping with it and baking it uncovered for five

further minutes. (9) Top with a side salad and serve hot.

20. Roasted Sweet Potatoes and Kale Salad

Total Time: 35 minutes | Prep Time: 10 minutes

Ingredients:

- 2 large sweet potatoes, peeled and diced
- 2 tablespoons olive oil
- 1 teaspoon smoked paprika
- ½ teaspoon salt
- ½ teaspoon black pepper
- 4 cups chopped kale
- ¼ cup dried cranberries
- ¼ cup crumbled goat cheese
- ¼ cup toasted pecans
- 2 tablespoons balsamic vinegar
- 1 tablespoon Dijon mustard
- 1 tablespoon honey

Directions:

(1) Bring the steam oven up to temperature, then set it to combined steam-roasting mode. (2) A tablespoon of olive oil, some paprika, salt, and black pepper should be mixed with the sweet potatoes. (3) Roast for 20 minutes or until soft, spread out on a baking sheet. (4) As a side note, to soften the kale, massage it with the remaining olive oil for 1-2 minutes. (5) In a small bowl, blend together the balsamic vinegar, honey, & Dijon mustard to make the dressing. Blend together kale, roasted sweet potatoes, cranberries, goat cheese, and nuts in a dish. (6) You may serve it warm or at room temperature; pour dressing over it.

21. Greek Salad with Lemon Vinaigrette

Total Time: 15 minutes | Prep Time: 15 minutes

Ingredients:

- 1 cucumber, diced
- 1 cup cherry tomatoes, halved
- ½ red onion, thinly sliced
- ½ cup Kalamata olives, pitted and halved
- 1 cup feta cheese, crumbled
- 2 tbsp fresh parsley, chopped
- For the Lemon Vinaigrette:
- 3 tbsp olive oil
- 1 tbsp fresh lemon juice
- 1 tsp Dijon mustard
- 1 clove garlic, minced
- ½ tsp dried oregano
- Salt and pepper to taste

Directions:

(1) Shake up the feta cheese, olives, cherry tomatoes, red onion, and cucumber in a big basin. (2) Combine the olive oil, oregano, garlic, lemon juice, Dijon mustard, salt, & pepper in a little dish and whisk to combine. (3) Toss the salad lightly to blend after drizzling the dressing over it. (4) Serve immediately after garnishing with fresh parsley.

22. Greek Quinoa and Chickpea Salad

Total Time: 20 minutes | Prep Time: 10 minutes | Cook Time: 10 minutes

Ingredients:

- 1 cup quinoa, rinsed
- 2 cups water

1 can chickpeas, drained & rinsed	1 cup cherry tomatoes, halved
½ cucumber, diced	½ red onion, finely chopped
½ cup feta cheese, crumbled	¼ cup fresh parsley, chopped
For the Dressing:	3 tbsp olive oil
1 tbsp red wine vinegar	1 tsp dried oregano
Salt and pepper to taste	

Directions:

(1) Steam oven temperature should be set at 212°F or 100°C. (2) To make fluffy quinoa, combine water and quinoa in a steam-safe dish and simmer for 10 minutes. Allow to cool. (3) Mix the cooked quinoa, chickpeas, cherry tomatoes, cucumber, red onion, and feta in a big basin. (4) Marge olive oil, red wine vinegar, oregano, salt, & pepper in a little dish & whisk to combine. (5) Toss the salad to combine, then top with dressing and fresh parsley.

23. Chicken and Broccoli Alfredo

Total Time: 30 minutes | Prep Time: 10 minutes | Cook Time: 20 minutes

Ingredients:

Stripped chicken breasts that have been deboned and skinned	2 cups broccoli florets
8 oz fettuccine pasta	2 tbsp olive oil
2 cloves garlic, minced	1 cup heavy cream
½ cup grated Parmesan cheese	Salt and pepper to taste

Directions:

(1) Set the steam oven to 212°F, which is 100°C. (2) Fill a steam-safe dish halfway with water and add the pasta. Cook in a steamer for 12 minutes or until the pasta reaches the desired texture of crispiness. Reserve the drained liquid. (3) Cook the chicken for 12 minutes in a separate pan, and then add the broccoli after 6 minutes to cook for another 6 minutes. (4) As a side note, in a skillet over medium heat, warm the olive oil. Sauté the garlic for 1 minute after adding it. (5) Creamy Parmesan and heavy cream should be stirred in. Simmer un till the mixture thickens, about three minutes. (6) Toss in the spaghetti, broccoli, and steamed chicken with the sauce. Add salt & pepper, toss to combine, and serve right away.

24. Sweet Potato & Black Bean Tacos

Total Time: 25 minutes | Prep Time: 10 minutes | Cook Time: 15 minutes

Ingredients:

2 medium sweet potatoes, peeled and diced	1 can black beans, drained & rinsed
1 tsp cumin	½ tsp smoked paprika
Salt and pepper to taste	8 small corn tortillas
½ cup crumbled feta or cotija cheese	¼ cup chopped fresh cilantro
1 avocado, sliced	

Directions:

(1) Steam oven temperature should be set at 212°F or 100°C. (2) Cook the sweet potatoes in a steamer for about 15 minutes or until they are soft. (3) Black beans, cumin, smoked paprika, salt, & pepper should be tossed with the cooked sweet potatoes in a bowl. (4) For a minute, reheat the tortillas in the steam oven.

(5) Before topping with cheese, cilantro, and avocado slices, layer the tacos with the black bean and sweet potato filling. (6) Garnish with lime wedges & serve right away.

25. Balsamic Roasted Carrots

Total Time: 20 minutes | Prep Time: 5 minutes | Cook Time: 15 minutes

Ingredients:

1 lb baby carrots	2 tbsp balsamic vinegar
1 tbsp olive oil	1 tsp honey
½ tsp dried thyme	Salt and pepper to taste

Directions:

(1) Steam oven temperature should be set at 212°F or 100°C. (2) Toss the olive oil, balsamic vinegar, honey, thyme, salt, & pepper in a bowl & whisk to combine. (3) Stir the carrots into the balsamic glaze. (4) Steam for 15 minutes, stirring once, in a pan that can withstand steam. (5) Warm it up and put it on the side.

26. Garlic Herb Chicken Wings

Total Time: 40 minutes | Prep Time: 10 minutes

Ingredients:

2 lbs chicken wings	2 tbsp olive oil
4 cloves garlic, minced	1 tsp dried oregano
1 tsp dried thyme	1 tsp dried rosemary
½ tsp salt	½ tsp black pepper
½ tsp paprika	1 tbsp lemon juice
Chopped fresh parsley for garnish	

Directions:

(1) Switch to combined steam mode and heat the steam oven to 375°F, or 190°C. (2) Combine olive oil, garlic, oregano, thyme, rosemary, salt, pepper, and paprika in a big bowl; then, add the chicken wings & mix to coat. (3) Place a sturdy tray below the wings to collect any drips, then arrange them in a single layer on a steam oven tray with holes in them. (4) After 25 minutes of steaming, set the oven to 400°F, or 205°C, and roast for 10-15 more minutes, or until crispy. (5) Serve heated with a squeeze of lemon juice and some fresh parsley for garnish.

27. Broccoli and Cheddar Stuffed Chicken

Total Time: 45 minutes | Prep Time: 15 minutes

Ingredients:

2 large boneless, skinless chicken breasts	1 cup broccoli, finely chopped
½ cup shredded cheddar cheese	1 clove garlic, minced
½ tsp salt	½ tsp black pepper
½ tsp paprika	1 tbsp olive oil

Directions:

(1) Switch to combined steam mode and heat the steam oven to 375°F, or 190°C. (2) Avoid slicing through the chicken breasts as you cut a pocket into them. (3) Throw the broccoli, cheddar cheese, garlic, salt, and pepper into a bowl and stir. Place the chicken breasts with this filling in the middle. (4) Apply paprika and olive oil to the chicken. (5) After the chicken reaches an internal heat of 74°C, take it out of the oven and put it on a steam oven tray to cook for another 30-35 minutes. Allow to sit for a

few while before cutting. Keep heated before serving.

28. Lemon Dill Roasted Potatoes

Total Time: 35 minutes | Prep Time: 10 minutes

Ingredients:

1.5 lbs baby potatoes, halved	2 tbsp olive oil
1 tbsp lemon juice	1 tsp lemon zest
1 tsp dried dill	½ tsp salt
½ tsp black pepper	2 cloves garlic, minced

Directions:

(1) The steam oven should be preheated to 400°F, or 205°C, using the combined steam setting. (2) Olive oil, garlic, lemon zest, dill, salt, and pepper should be mixed with the potatoes. (3) Arrange evenly on a steam oven baking sheet. (4) To get a golden brown color and tenderness, roast for 25 to 30 minutes. (5) As a side dish, serve warm.

29. Greek Quinoa and Feta Salad

Total Time: 20 minutes | Prep Time: 10 minutes

Ingredients:

1 cup quinoa	2 cups water
1 cup cherry tomatoes, halved	½ cucumber, diced
¼ red onion, finely chopped	¼ cup Kalamata olives, sliced
½ cup feta cheese, crumbled	2 tbsp olive oil
1 tbsp red wine vinegar	1 tsp dried oregano
Salt and pepper to taste	

Directions:

(1) In a steam-safe dish, combine the quinoa and water. Steam for 15 minutes at 212°F or 100°C. Do not fluff with a fork un till cooled. (2) Toss the quinoa with the cucumber, feta, olives, cherry tomatoes, red onion, and a big bowl. (3) Combine the oregano, salt, pepper, red wine vinegar, olive oil, and a small bowl and whisk to combine. (4) Toss the salad to blend after pouring the dressing over it. (5) Whether served cold or warm, the choice is yours.

30. Lemon Dill Chicken Skewers

Total Time: 30 minutes | Prep Time: 15 minutes

Ingredients:

Two cubed breasts of chicken that have been boneless and skinless	2 tbsp olive oil
1 tbsp lemon juice	1 tsp lemon zest
1 tsp dried dill	½ tsp salt
½ tsp black pepper	½ tsp garlic powder
Wooden skewers soaked in water	

Directions:

(1) Set the steam oven to combined steam and heat it to 375°F, or 190°C. (2) For the dressing, gather all the ingredients in a bowl: olive oil, lemon juice, zest, dill, salt, pepper, and garlic powder. Toss in the chicken cubes and coat them. Set aside to soak for ten minutes. (3) Skewer the chicken once it has been soaked. (4) The chicken should attain an internal heat

of 74°C after 15 to 20 minutes of cooking on a steam oven tray, with a flip every 5 minutes. (5) Pair it with some tzatziki or a crisp salad for a side dish.

31. Lemon Garlic Herb Shrimp

Total Time: 15 minutes | Prep Time: 10 minutes

Ingredients:

- 1 lb large shrimp, peeled and deveined
- 2 tbsp olive oil
- 3 cloves garlic, minced
- 1 tbsp fresh lemon juice
- 1 tsp lemon zest
- 1 tbsp fresh parsley, chopped
- 1 tsp dried oregano
- Salt and pepper to taste

Directions:

(1) Steam oven temperature should be set at 375°F or 190°C. (2) The ingredients for the dressing include garlic, olive oil, lemon zest and juice, parsley, oregano, salt, and pepper. (3) Coat the shrimp well in the marinade by tossing them around. (4) Arrange the shrimp in a dish that can withstand steam. (5) After 6 to 8 minutes of steaming in the oven, the shrimp should be opaque and pink. (6) Garnish with more parsley & lemon wedges, & serve right away.

32. Mediterranean Roasted Chickpeas

Total Time: 25 minutes | Prep Time: 10 minutes

Ingredients:

- 2 cans (15 oz each) chickpeas, drained and rinsed
- 2 tbsp olive oil
- 1 tsp smoked paprika
- 1 tsp garlic powder
- 1 tsp dried oregano
- 1/2 tsp cumin
- Salt and pepper to taste
- Fresh parsley for garnish

Directions:

(1) Turn the steam oven's convection heat setting up to 400°F or 200°C. (2) To eliminate any surplus of moisture, gently pat the chickpeas dry using paper towels. (3) Combine the chickpeas with the olive oil, onion powder, cumin, garlic powder, oregano, and pepper in a bowl. (4) On a baking sheet that can withstand steam, spread the chickpeas evenly. (5) After 20 to 25 minutes of roasting, shake the pan halfway through to distribute the chickpeas evenly. (6) Serve after removing from oven and topping with fresh parsley.

33. Lemon Herb Rice

Total Time: 30 minutes | Prep Time: 10 minutes

Ingredients:

- 1 cup long-grain rice
- 2 cups vegetable broth
- 1 tbsp olive oil
- 1 tsp lemon zest
- 1 tbsp fresh lemon juice
- 1 tbsp fresh parsley, chopped
- Salt to taste

Directions:

(1) Steam oven temperature should be set at 375°F or 190°C. (2) After washing the rice in cold water, make sure the water is clear. (3) Throw the rice, veggie stock, olive oil, salt, lemon zest, and steam-safe dish into the oven. (4) Before placing the dish in the oven, cover it with aluminum foil or a lid. (5) Cook the rice in a steamer for 20 to 25 minutes or until it absorbs all of the liquid. (6) When ready to

serve, fluff the rice with a fork and whisk in the lemon juice. Top with parsley.

34. Garlic Parmesan Roasted Broccoli

Total Time: 20 minutes | Prep Time: 10 minutes

Ingredients:

1 lb broccoli florets	2 tbsp olive oil
3 cloves garlic, minced	1/2 cup grated Parmesan cheese
1/2 tsp red pepper flakes (optional)	Salt and pepper to taste

Directions:

(1) Bring the convection temperature of the steam oven up to 400°F, or 200°C. (2) The broccoli florets should be mixed in a basin with garlic, olive oil, salt, and pepper. (3) When baking in a steam oven, make sure to spread the broccoli out evenly. (4) To get a soft and somewhat crunchy texture, roast in a steam oven for around fifteen to twenty minutes. (5) Before serving it hot, take it out of the oven and top it with Parmesan and red pepper flakes.

35. Baked Teriyaki Tofu

Total Time: 40 minutes | Prep Time: 15 minutes

Ingredients:

One block of firm tofu pressed & cut into cubes	1/4 cup soy sauce
2 tbsp honey or maple syrup	2 tbsp rice vinegar
1 tbsp sesame oil	1 clove garlic, minced
1 tsp grated ginger	1 tbsp sesame seeds
2 green onions, sliced	

Directions:

(1) Before using, bring the steam oven up to a temperature of 190°C. (2) To prepare the marinade, combine the following ingredients in a bowl: rice vinegar, soy sauce, honey, garlic, and ginger. Whisk in the sesame oil. (3) Marinate the tofu cubes for 10 minutes after tossing them in the sauce. (4) After 25 to 30 minutes of steaming, the tofu should be brown and somewhat crunchy. (5) Garnish with chopped green onions & sesame seeds just before dining.

36. Lemon Garlic Roasted Mushrooms

Total Time: 25 minutes | Prep Time: 10 minutes

Ingredients:

1 lb (450g) cremini or button mushrooms, cleaned and halved	3 tbsp olive oil
3 cloves garlic, minced	1 tbsp lemon juice
1 tsp lemon zest	1/2 tsp salt
1/2 tsp black pepper	1/2 tsp dried thyme
1 tbsp chopped fresh parsley	

Directions:

(1) Switch to combined steam mode and heat the steam oven to 375°F, or 190°C. (2) Combine the mushrooms with the garlic, olive oil, lemon zest, juice, salt, pepper, and thyme in a big bowl. (3) Arrange the mushrooms in a uniform layer on a baking pan. (4) Stir occasionally while roasting for 15 minutes in a steam oven. (5) After taking it out of the oven,

top it with chopped fresh parsley and enjoy it warm.

37. Mediterranean Stuffed Zucchini

Total Time: 35 minutes | Prep Time: 15 minutes

Ingredients:

- 3 medium zucchinis, halved lengthwise and hollowed out
- 1/4 cup feta cheese, crumbled
- 2 tbsp black olives, chopped
- 1 clove garlic, minced
- Salt and pepper to taste
- 1/2 cup cooked quinoa
- 1/4 cup cherry tomatoes, diced
- 1 tbsp olive oil
- 1/2 tsp dried oregano
- 1 tbsp chopped fresh basil

Directions:

(1) Get the steam oven preheated to 375°F, or 190°C, and set it to steam-bake mode. (2) Throw all the ingredients into a dish and stir in the quinoa, feta, cherry tomatoes, olives, garlic, oregano, salt, and pepper. (3) Fill the zucchini halves with the filling and set them on a baking dish that can withstand steam. (4) Zucchini should be cooked until soft, around 20 minutes, in a steam oven. (5) Take it out, top it with chopped basil, and serve it hot.

38. Thai Peanut Chicken

Total Time: 30 minutes | Prep Time: 10 minutes

Ingredients:

- Stripped chicken breasts that have been deboned and skinned
- 1/2 cup coconut milk
- 2 tbsp peanut butter
- 1 tbsp lime juice
- 1 tsp grated ginger
- 1/2 tsp red pepper flakes (optional)
- 1 tbsp chopped cilantro (for garnish)
- 1 tbsp soy sauce
- 1 tsp honey
- 1 clove garlic, minced
- 2 tbsp chopped peanuts (for garnish)

Directions:

(1) Turn the steam oven on to 300°F (150°C) to heat it up. (2) The ingredients—coconut milk, peanut butter, soy sauce, lime juice, honey, ginger, garlic, and red pepper flakes—must be amalgamated in a basin. (3) Before steaming, coat the chicken strips with the peanut sauce. (4) The chicken should be cooked thoroughly after 20 minutes of steaming. (5) Serve with chopped peanuts and cilantro as a garnish.

39. Greek Chicken and Rice Salad

Total Time: 35 minutes | Prep Time: 15 minutes

Ingredients:

- 1 cup cooked jasmine or basmati rice
- 1/4 cup cherry tomatoes, halved
- 1/4 cup Kalamata olives, sliced
- 2 tbsp olive oil
- 1 tsp dried oregano
- 1 tbsp chopped fresh parsley
- 1 cup cooked shredded chicken
- 1/4 cup cucumber, diced
- 1/4 cup feta cheese, crumbled
- 1 tbsp lemon juice
- Salt and pepper to taste

Directions:

(1) Set the steam oven to 350°F (175°C) before cooking. (2) In a dish that can withstand steam, combine the rice and chicken shreds. (3) Cook the chicken and rice in a steamer for 10 minutes or until they are cooked completely. (4) After taking it out of the steamer, combine the squash, cucumber, olives, feta, lemon juice, oregano, salt, and pepper with the olive oil. (5) Add some parsley for garnish and enjoy warm or room temperature.

40. Lemon Garlic Roasted Salmon

Total Time: 20 minutes | Prep Time: 5 minutes

Ingredients:

2 salmon fillets	2 tbsp olive oil
2 cloves garlic, minced	1 tbsp lemon juice
1 tsp lemon zest	1/2 tsp salt
1/2 tsp black pepper	1/2 tsp dried dill
1 tbsp chopped fresh parsley	

Directions:

(1) Turn the steam oven's combined steam setting to 400°F (200°C). (2) In a petite basin, combine the dill, garlic, lemon zest, juice, salt, and olive oil. (3) After brushing the salmon fillets with the mixture, set them on a baking sheet that can withstand steam. (4) Cook the salmon in a steam oven for 12–15 minutes or until it flakes easily. (5) After taking it out of the oven, sprinkle some parsley on top and serve it warm.

41. Roasted Stuffed Eggplant

Total Time: 50 minutes | Prep Time: 15 minutes

Ingredients:

2 medium eggplants, halved lengthwise	1 cup cherry tomatoes, diced
1/2 cup cooked quinoa	1/4 cup feta cheese, crumbled
1/4 cup fresh parsley, chopped	2 cloves garlic, minced
1 tbsp olive oil	1 tsp dried oregano
Salt and pepper, to taste	

Directions:

(1) Set the steam oven to combined steam mode and heat it to 375°F, or 190°C. (2) Remove the eggplant flesh from both halves, being sure to leave a 1/4-inch border around each. Chop the meat and set it aside in a basin. (3) Parsley, quinoa, feta, olive oil, oregano, salt, pepper, garlic, and tomatoes should be added. Blend well. (4) Spoon the filling into the eggplant halves & set them on a baking sheet. (5) Cook the eggplant and filling in a steam oven for 30–35 minutes or until softened and brown. (6) Top with more feta and parsley, and serve warm.

42. Sweet Potato and Black Bean Salad

Total Time: 30 minutes | Prep Time: 10 minutes

Ingredients:

2 medium sweet potatoes, peeled and diced	1 can black beans, drained & rinsed
1/4 cup red onion, finely chopped	1/4 cup cilantro, chopped
1/4 cup feta cheese, crumbled (optional)	1 tbsp olive oil
1 tbsp lime juice	1/2 tsp cumin

| 1/2 tsp smoked paprika | Salt and pepper, to taste |

Directions:

(1) Start the steam oven at 210°F, or 100°C, using the steam setting. (2) To make the sweet potatoes soft, steam them for 15 minutes on a perforated steam tray and dice them. (3) The black beans, red onion, and cilantro should be mixed together in a big basin. (4) Lime juice, cumin, smoked paprika, olive oil, salt, and pepper should be whisked together in a small bowl. (5) Before tossing with the dressing, add the cooked sweet potatoes to the bowl. (6) If used, garnish with feta cheese. Have it warm or cold.

43. Greek Quinoa and Chickpea Bowl

Total Time: 35 minutes | Prep Time: 15 minutes

Ingredients:

1 cup quinoa, rinsed	1 3/4 cups water
1 can chickpeas, drained & rinsed	1/2 cup cucumber, diced
1/2 cup cherry tomatoes, halved	1/4 cup kalamata olives, sliced
1/4 cup feta cheese, crumbled	2 tbsp olive oil
1 tbsp lemon juice	1 tsp dried oregano
Salt and pepper, to taste	

Directions:

(1) Turn the steam oven on to 210 degrees Fahrenheit (100 degrees Celsius). (2) Bring the water and quinoa to a boil in a saucepan. After 20 minutes of steaming, the water should have been absorbed. (3) Toss the quinoa with a fork when it has cooled a little. (4) Quinoa, chickpeas, cucumber, tomatoes, olives, and feta should all be mixed together in a big basin. (5) Combine the oregano, olive oil, lemon juice, salt, & pepper in a little bowl & whisk to combine. Add the dressing to the salad & blend well. (6) You may serve it refrigerated or at room temperature.

44. Spaghetti with Creamy Mushroom Sauce

Total Time: 35 minutes | Prep Time: 10 minutes

Ingredients:

8 oz spaghetti	2 cups cremini mushrooms, sliced
2 cloves garlic, minced	1 cup heavy cream
1/2 cup vegetable broth	1/4 cup Parmesan cheese, grated
1 tbsp olive oil	1 tsp dried thyme
Salt and pepper, to taste	Fresh parsley for garnish

Directions:

(1) Turn the steam oven on to 210 degrees Fahrenheit (100 degrees Celsius). (2) Fill a steam tray halfway with water and add the pasta. Cook in a steamer for 15 to 18 minutes or until the bite is just right. Reserve the drained liquid. (3) Melt the olive oil in a skillet set over middle heat. After 5 minutes of sautéing, add the garlic and mushrooms. (4) Add the veggie broth and reduce heat to low. To thicken the sauce, add the heavy cream and thyme and continue cooking for five more minutes. (5) Next, add the Parmesan, salt, and pepper and mix well. (6) Mix the pasta with the sauce & top with fresh parsley before serving.

45. Balsamic Roasted Veggies

Total Time: 40 minutes | Prep Time: 10 minutes

Ingredients:

1 zucchini, sliced	1 red bell pepper, sliced
1 yellow bell pepper, sliced	1 red onion, sliced
1 cup cherry tomatoes	2 tbsp balsamic vinegar
1 tbsp olive oil	1 tsp dried Italian herbs
Salt and pepper, to taste	

Directions:

(1) Use the combined steam setting to get the steam oven up to 375°F, or 190°C. (2) Combine cherry tomatoes, bell peppers, onion, balsamic vinegar, olive oil, Italian herbs, salt, and pepper in a big bowl. Add bell peppers, zucchini, and cherry tomatoes. (3) Put the vegetables in an equal layer on a baking pan. Cook in a steam oven for 25 to 30 minutes, tossing halfway through or until soft and browned. (4) Warm it up and serve it as a side, or top it with some grains for a full dinner.

46. Zucchini Noodles with Pesto

Total Time: 20 minutes | Prep Time: 10 minutes

Ingredients:

2 medium zucchini, spiralized	½ cup basil pesto (store-bought or homemade)
½ cup cherry tomatoes, halved	¼ cup Parmesan cheese, grated
1 tablespoon olive oil	½ teaspoon salt
¼ teaspoon black pepper	¼ teaspoon red pepper flakes (optional)

Directions:

(1) First, bring the temperature of the steam oven up to 200°F, which is 90°C. (2) Toss the spiralized zucchini with a steaming tray and cook for three to five minutes or until soft but not overdone. (3) Pasta, cherry tomatoes, cooked zucchini, pesto, olive oil, salt, and pepper should all be mixed together in a big basin. To coat, mix well. (4) Place on individual dishes and, if desired, garnish with Parmesan and red pepper flakes. (5) Indulge right now and savor!

47. Thai Coconut Curry Chicken

Total Time: 45 minutes | Prep Time: 15 minutes

Ingredients:

2 boneless, skinless chicken breasts	1 cup coconut milk
1 tablespoon red curry paste	1 tablespoon soy sauce
1 teaspoon fish sauce	1 teaspoon brown sugar
1 teaspoon grated ginger	1 clove garlic, minced
1 small red bell pepper, sliced	1 small zucchini, sliced
½ cup snap peas	½ cup chopped fresh cilantro

Directions:

(1) Make sure the steam oven is heated up to 350°F (175°C). (2) Combine all of the ingredients in a bowl and whisk until smooth. Add the red curry paste, soy sauce, fish sauce, brown sugar, ginger, and garlic. (3) Coat the chicken breasts with the coconut curry sauce & transfer them to a baking dish that can withstand steam. (4) Before adding the snap peas, bell pepper, and zucchini, steam for 25 minutes and add another 10 minutes of steaming time. (5) Take it out and set it aside to rest for five minutes. (6) Serve with steaming jasmine rice and garnish with fresh cilantro.

48. Lemon Herb Roasted Chicken and Veggies

Total Time: 50 minutes | Prep Time: 15 minutes

Ingredients:

1 whole chicken (about 4 lbs)	1 lemon, sliced
3 tablespoons olive oil	1 teaspoon salt
½ teaspoon black pepper	1 teaspoon dried thyme
1 teaspoon dried rosemary	2 cloves garlic, minced
1 cup baby carrots	1 cup Brussels sprouts, halved
1 cup baby potatoes, halved	

Directions:

(1) A steam oven should be preheated to 375°F, or 190°C. (2) Season the whole chicken with a mixture of olive oil, pepper, salt, rosemary, and chopped garlic. Add thyme and rosemary. Fill the cavity with slices of lemon. (3) Roast the chicken for 30 minutes in a roasting pan that is safe to use with steam. (4) Arrange the young potatoes, Brussels sprouts, carrots, and chicken in a circular pattern. Add more olive oil & toss to combine. (5) When the chicken reaches an internal heat of 75°C, remove it from the steamer and let it rest for another 15 to 20 minutes. (6) Allow to cool for ten minutes before carving. Pita bread and top with the roasted veggies.

49. Roasted Vegetable and Quinoa Bowl

Total Time: 35 minutes | Prep Time: 15 minutes

Ingredients:

1 cup quinoa, rinsed	2 cups water
1 small sweet potato, diced	1 cup broccoli florets
1 red bell pepper, sliced	½ red onion, sliced
2 tablespoons olive oil	½ teaspoon salt
¼ teaspoon black pepper	½ teaspoon smoked paprika
½ teaspoon garlic powder	¼ cup feta cheese, crumbled
2 tablespoons chopped fresh parsley	

Directions:

(1) A steam oven should be preheated to 375°F, or 190°C. (2) The quinoa and water should be combined in a saucepan that can withstand steam. Continue steaming for another 20 minutes or until the vegetables are soft. Use a fork to fluff. (3) In a large bowl, marge the sweet potato, broccoli, bell pepper, red onion, and smoked paprika. Season with salt & pepper, then whisk in the garlic powder, olive oil, and salt. (4) Roast the veggies in a steam oven for 20 minutes after spreading them out

on a steaming tray. (5) Top each dish with quinoa and roasted veggies. Garnish with chopped fresh parsley & crumbled feta. Keep heated before serving.

50. Lemon Garlic Pork Chops

Total Time: 35 minutes | Prep Time: 10 minutes

Ingredients:

- 2 bone-in pork chops
- 2 tablespoons olive oil
- 1 teaspoon salt
- ½ teaspoon black pepper
- 1 teaspoon garlic powder
- 1 teaspoon dried oregano
- 1 lemon, sliced
- 2 cloves garlic, minced
- ½ cup chicken broth

Directions:

(1) Make sure the steam oven is heated up to 350°F (175°C). (2) Spice up your pork chops with a rub of oregano, garlic powder, salt, and pepper. (3) Toss the pork chops into a steam-proof baking tray. On top, sprinkle with minced garlic and lemon wedges. Whisk in the chicken stock. (4) Bring the pork to an internal heat of 145°F, or 63°C, after 25-30 minutes of steaming. (5) Allow to cool for five minutes before consumption. As a side dish, try mashed potatoes or steamed veggies.

51. Lemon Herb Baked Salmon

Total Time: 25 minutes | Prep Time: 10 minutes

Ingredients:

- 4 salmon fillets (6 oz each)
- 2 tbsp olive oil
- 2 tbsp fresh lemon juice
- 1 tsp lemon zest
- 2 cloves garlic, minced
- 1 tsp dried oregano
- 1 tsp dried thyme
- ½ tsp salt
- ½ tsp black pepper
- 4 lemon slices
- 2 tbsp fresh parsley, chopped

Directions:

(1) Turn the steam oven's combined steam setting to 350°F (175°C) to get it hot. (2) Marge the olive oil, lemon zest & juice, garlic, oregano, thyme, salt, & pepper in a little bowl. (3) After brushing the salmon fillets with the herb mixture, set them on a baking tray. Slice one lemon and place it on top of each fillet. (4) After 12–15 minutes of steam baking, the salmon should be opaque and flake readily when tested with a fork. (5) Serve heated with a sprinkle of fresh parsley for garnish.

52. Chicken Cacciatore

Total Time: 50 minutes | Prep Time: 15 minutes

Ingredients:

- 4 bone-in, skin-on chicken thighs
- 2 tbsp olive oil
- 1 small onion, diced
- 2 cloves garlic, minced
- 1 red bell pepper, sliced
- 1 cup diced tomatoes (canned or fresh)
- ½ cup chicken broth
- ½ cup dry red wine
- 1 tsp dried oregano
- 1 tsp dried basil
- ½ tsp salt
- ½ tsp black pepper

¼ tsp red pepper flakes (optional)

2 tbsp fresh parsley, chopped

¼ cup black olives, sliced

Directions:

(1) Turn on the steam-bake function of the steam oven and heat it to 375°F, or 190°C. (2) In a skillet set over middle heat, warm the olive oil. When the chicken thighs are golden brown, sear them for three to four minutes on each side. (3) Place the chicken on a baking sheet. Cook the bell pepper, onions, and garlic for two or three minutes in the same pan. (4) Season with salt, pepper, oregano, basil, wine, chicken broth, and red pepper flakes. Add tomatoes and stir in. Bring to a simmer and cook for five minutes. (5) Before steam-baking for 30–35 minutes, coat the chicken with the sauce. Cook till done. (6) Add the olives, stir, and top with the parsley before serving.

53. Spinach and Goat Cheese Stuffed Chicken

Total Time: 40 minutes | Prep Time: 15 minutes

Ingredients:

2 large boneless, skinless chicken breasts

½ cup goat cheese, crumbled

½ tsp dried oregano

½ tsp black pepper

1 cup fresh spinach, chopped

1 clove garlic, minced

½ tsp salt

1 tbsp olive oil

Directions:

(1) Get the steam oven up to temperature, using the combined steam setting, at least 375°F, or 190°C. (2) Make a shallow incision in the center of each chicken breast; do not cut through. (3) Combine goat cheese, spinach, garlic, oregano, salt, and pepper in a mixing bowl. Fill the chicken pockets with the filling. (4) After brushing the chicken with olive oil, use toothpicks to secure the opening. (5) Once the chicken has reached an internal heat of 74°C, transfer it to a baking dish and steam-bake it for 25-30 minutes. (6) Before serving, take the toothpicks out.

54. Spinach and Feta Stuffed Mushrooms

Total Time: 30 minutes | Prep Time: 10 minutes

Ingredients:

12 large white or cremini mushrooms, stems removed

½ cup feta cheese, crumbled

¼ tsp dried oregano

1 tbsp olive oil

1 cup fresh spinach, chopped

1 clove garlic, minced

¼ tsp black pepper

Directions:

(1) Bring the steam oven up to temperature, then set it to 350°F or 175°C. (2) Combine the feta cheese, spinach, garlic, oregano, and black pepper in a bowl. (3) Distribute the spinach-feta filling among the filled mushroom caps. Put a little olive oil on top. (4) Steam the mushrooms for around fifteen to twenty minutes after placing them on a baking sheet. (5) As a starter or a side dish, serve warm.

55. Roasted Sweet Potatoes with Cilantro

Total Time: 35 minutes | Prep Time: 10 minutes

Ingredients:

2 large sweet potatoes, peeled and cubed	2 tbsp olive oil
½ tsp salt	½ tsp black pepper
½ tsp smoked paprika	½ tsp ground cumin
2 tbsp fresh cilantro, chopped	

Directions:

(1) Turn the steam oven's combined steam setting up to 400°F, or 200°C. (2) Combine sweet potatoes, olive oil, salt, pepper, cumin, and paprika in a mixing bowl. (3) Pour the batter onto an even baking pan layer. (4) Cook in a steam oven for 25 to 30 minutes, tossing halfway through or until soft and browned. (5) Before serving, top with chopped fresh cilantro.

56. Thai Peanut Chicken Salad

Total Time: 35 minutes | Prep Time: 15 minutes | Cook Time: 20 minutes

Ingredients:

2 boneless, skinless chicken breasts	1 cup shredded red cabbage
1 cup shredded carrots	1/2 cup chopped cucumber
1/2 cup chopped red bell pepper	1/4 cup chopped fresh cilantro
1/4 cup chopped peanuts	1/4 cup green onions, sliced
1/4 cup peanut butter	2 tbsp soy sauce
1 tbsp rice vinegar	1 tbsp lime juice
1 tbsp honey	1 tsp sesame oil
1/2 tsp grated ginger	1/2 tsp minced garlic

Directions:

(1) Start the steam oven at 212 degrees Fahrenheit (100 degrees Celsius). (2) Lay the chicken breasts on a steam tray with holes in it. Before serving, steam for 18 to 20 minutes to ensure doneness. After a short cooling period, chop them. (3) Throw all the ingredients—carrots, cucumber, red bell pepper, cilantro, peanuts, and green onions—into a big bowl and mix well. (4) To prepare the dressing, combine peanut butter, soy sauce, rice vinegar, lime juice, honey, sesame oil, ginger, and garlic in a small bowl. Whisk to combine. (5) After you've mixed the salad with the peanut dressing, add the shredded chicken. Quickly prepare and serve.

57. Greek Chicken and Rice

Total Time: 40 minutes | Prep Time: 10 minutes | Cook Time: 30 minutes

Ingredients:

2 boneless, skinless chicken breasts	1 cup jasmine rice
1 ½ cups chicken broth	1/2 cup cherry tomatoes, halved
1/2 cup chopped cucumber	1/4 cup crumbled feta cheese
1/4 cup sliced kalamata olives	1 tbsp olive oil
1 tbsp lemon juice	1 tsp dried oregano
1/2 tsp garlic powder	Salt and pepper to taste

Directions:

(1) Start the steam oven at 212 degrees Fahrenheit (100 degrees Celsius). (2) Mix the jasmine rice with the chicken broth in a dish that can withstand steam. Cook on high heat for a duration of 20 minutes. (3) For the chicken

breasts, season with salt, pepper, garlic powder, lemon juice, oregano, and olive oil. Set them on a steam tray with holes in it and cook them for 25 minutes. (4) After cooking is complete, set aside 5 minutes to rest before slicing. (5) After the rice is cooked, fluff it and combine it with cucumber, feta cheese, olives, and cherry tomatoes. (6) Place the cut chicken on top of the Greek rice mixture and serve.

58. Creamy Avocado and Spinach Pasta

Total Time: 30 minutes | Prep Time: 10 minutes | Cook Time: 20 minutes

Ingredients:

8 oz whole wheat pasta	1 ripe avocado
1 cup fresh spinach	1/2 cup plain Greek yogurt
1/4 cup grated Parmesan cheese	2 tbsp olive oil
1 tbsp lemon juice	1 clove garlic, minced
Salt and pepper to taste	1/4 cup chopped fresh basil (optional)

Directions:

(1) On steam mode, bring the steam oven up to 212°F, or 100°C. (2) Steam the pasta for around fifteen to twenty minutes, or until it reaches the desired doneness (al dente), in a steam-safe dish. Reserve the drained liquid. (3) Add the avocado, spinach, Greek yogurt, Parmesan, olive oil, lemon juice, garlic, salt, & pepper to a blender. Blend until smooth. Puree the mixture. (4) Combine the spaghetti and sauce, then toss in the avocado-spinach mixture. (5) Warm the dish before topping it with fresh basil.

59. Roasted Cauliflower Rice

Total Time: 25 minutes | Prep Time: 10 minutes | Cook Time: 15 minutes

Ingredients:

1 head cauliflower, cut into florets	1 tbsp olive oil
1/2 tsp garlic powder	1/2 tsp smoked paprika
1/2 tsp salt	1/4 tsp black pepper
1 tbsp chopped fresh parsley	

Directions:

(1) Start the steam oven at 212 degrees Fahrenheit (100 degrees Celsius). (2) Make rice-like florets from the cauliflower by pulsing them in a food processor. (3) Steam the cauliflower rice for 10 minutes after spreading it out on a steam-safe dish. (4) After the cauliflower rice has steamed, place it in a bowl and blend in the olive oil, garlic powder, smoked paprika, salt, & pepper. (5) To get a somewhat crunchy texture, roast for 5 minutes in a steam oven set to combination mode (steam + convection @ 375°F). (6) Before serving, top with fresh parsley.

60. Spicy Roasted Sweet Potatoes

Total Time: 35 minutes | Prep Time: 10 minutes | Cook Time: 25 minutes

Ingredients:

2 large sweet potatoes, peeled and cubed	1 tbsp olive oil
1/2 tsp chili powder	1/2 tsp smoked paprika

1/2 tsp cumin	1/4 tsp cayenne pepper
1/2 tsp salt	1/4 tsp black pepper
1 tbsp chopped fresh cilantro	

Directions:

(1) Start the steam oven at 212 degrees Fahrenheit (100 degrees Celsius). (2) Cook the sweet potatoes in a steamer for 10 minutes or until they are just soft. (3) Toss the cooked sweet potatoes in a big bowl with olive oil, salt, pepper, cumin, paprika, smoked, and chili powder. (4) After seasoning the potatoes, place them on a roasting sheet and bake them for 15 minutes at 400°F in the steam oven's combination mode (steam + convection). They should be somewhat crispy. (5) Serve heated with a sprinkle of fresh cilantro.

61. Herb-Crusted Salmon

Total Time: 25 minutes | Prep Time: 10 minutes

Ingredients:

4 salmon fillets (6 oz each)	2 tbsp Dijon mustard
½ cup panko breadcrumbs	¼ cup grated Parmesan cheese
2 tbsp fresh parsley, chopped	1 tbsp fresh dill, chopped
1 tbsp olive oil	1 tsp garlic powder
½ tsp salt	½ tsp black pepper
Lemon wedges (for serving)	

Directions:

(1) Bring the steam oven up to a temperature of 375°F, or 190°C, using the steam-bake function. (2) Before placing the salmon fillets on a baking sheet coated with paper, be sure to pat them dry. (3) Make sure to coat each fillet equally with Dijon mustard. (4) Put the panko breadcrumbs, Parmesan, dill, parsley, olive oil, garlic powder, salt, & black pepper in a small bowl. (5) Coat the mustard-coated side of the salmon with the breadcrumb mixture and press it down. (6) Once the crust has become golden brown and the salmon is flaky, transfer the pan to the steam oven and cook for 12–15 minutes. (7) Warm and garnish with lemon wedges.

62. Sweet Potato Fries

Total Time: 30 minutes | Prep Time: 10 minutes

Ingredients:

2 large sweet potatoes, peeled & cut into thin fries	1 tbsp cornstarch
1 tbsp olive oil	½ tsp smoked paprika
½ tsp garlic powder	½ tsp salt
¼ tsp black pepper	¼ tsp cayenne pepper (optional)

Directions:

(1) Turn the steam oven's combo steam-roast setting to 400°F (200°C). (2) Cornstarch may be used to crisp up sweet potato fries, so throw them in a big dish with them. (3) Olive oil should be drizzled over the top, followed by paprika, garlic powder, salt, black pepper, and cayenne, if used. Coat evenly by tossing. (4) Arrange the fries in an even layer on a parchment-lined baking sheet. (5) To get a golden brown color and crispy edges, steam-roast for 20 minutes, turning once halfway through. (6) Garnish with a dipping sauce of your choice and serve hot.

63. Mediterranean Baked Fish

Total Time: 35 minutes | Prep Time: 10 minutes

Ingredients:

Four white fish fillets (such as cod or halibut)	1 cup cherry tomatoes, halved
½ cup Kalamata olives, pitted and sliced	¼ cup red onion, thinly sliced
2 tbsp capers	2 tbsp olive oil
1 tbsp fresh lemon juice	1 tsp dried oregano
½ tsp salt	½ tsp black pepper
¼ cup crumbled feta cheese	Fresh basil for garnish

Directions:

(1) Get the steam oven preheated to 375°F, or 190°C, and set it to steam-bake mode. (2) Prepare a baking dish and add the fish fillets. (3) Combine the following ingredients in a bowl: cherry tomatoes, red onion, capers, olive oil, lemon juice, oregano, salt, and black pepper. (4) Pour the sauce over the fish in a uniform layer. (5) After ten to fifteen minutes of steam baking, the fish should be opaque and flake readily. (6) Prior to serving, top with crumbled feta and fresh basil.

64. Creamy Lemon Chicken Pasta

Total Time: 40 minutes | Prep Time: 10 minutes

Ingredients:

2 sliced chicken breasts that have been boneless and skinless	8 oz penne pasta
1 tbsp olive oil	2 cloves garlic, minced
1 cup chicken broth	1 cup heavy cream
½ cup grated Parmesan cheese	2 tbsp fresh lemon juice
1 tsp lemon zest	½ tsp salt
½ tsp black pepper	¼ tsp red pepper flakes (optional)
2 tbsp fresh parsley, chopped	

Directions:

(1) Put the steam oven on combined steam-bake mode and heat it up to 350°F (175°C). (2) Toss the pasta with the boiling water and transfer to a baking dish that can withstand steam. Cook until softened, about ten minutes, then remove from steam. (3) Brown the chicken in a skillet with heated olive oil. Sauté the garlic for 1 minute after adding it. (4) Simmer after adding chicken broth. (5) Add the heavy cream, Parmesan, lemon zest, salt, black pepper, red pepper flakes, & lemon juice. Stir well. (6) Coat the spaghetti with the sauce and toss it to combine. (7) After 15 minutes of baking in the steam oven, the mixture should be thick and creamy. (8) Warm and top with fresh parsley.

65. Teriyaki Glazed Tofu

Total Time: 30 minutes | Prep Time: 10 minutes

Ingredients:

1 block (14 oz) firm tofu, drained and cubed	2 tbsp cornstarch
1 tbsp sesame oil	½ cup teriyaki sauce

1 tbsp honey or maple syrup	1 tsp fresh ginger, grated
1 clove garlic, minced	1 tsp sesame seeds
2 green onions, sliced	

Directions:

(1) Put the steam oven on combined steam-roast mode and heat it up to 375°F, or 190°C. (2) To make tofu cubes crunchier, coat them with cornstarch. (3) Toss the tofu with sesame oil and place it on a baking sheet that has been prepared. (4) Turn once throughout the 20-minute steam-roasting time. (5) Put the ginger, garlic, honey, and teriyaki sauce in a small saucepan on medium heat. Bring to a simmer and cook for five minutes. (6) Before tossing the tofu with the teriyaki sauce, take it out of the oven. (7) Before serving, garnish with green onions & sesame seeds.

66. Lemon Herb Stuffed Chicken

Total Time: 40 minutes | Prep Time: 15 minutes

Ingredients:

2 boneless, skinless chicken breasts	½ cup fresh spinach, chopped
¼ cup feta cheese, crumbled	1 tbsp fresh parsley, chopped
1 tbsp fresh basil, chopped	1 tsp lemon zest
1 tbsp olive oil	1 tsp garlic powder
½ tsp salt	½ tsp black pepper

Directions:

(1) A steam oven should be preheated to 375°F, or 190°C. (2) Make an incision on the side of every chicken breast. (3) Gather the spinach, feta, parsley, basil, and zest of the lemon into a bowl. Fill the chicken pockets with the filling. (4) Before seasoning the chicken with salt, pepper, and garlic powder, brush it with olive oil. (5) After 25 minutes of steaming, the chicken should be cooked to an internal heat of 75 degrees Celsius. (6) Allow to cool for five minutes before consumption.

67. Black Bean and Corn Salad

Total Time: 20 minutes | Prep Time: 10 minutes

Ingredients:

1 can black beans, drained & rinsed	One cup of corn kernels (fresh, canned, or frozen)
½ red bell pepper, diced	¼ cup red onion, finely chopped
2 tbsp fresh cilantro, chopped	1 tbsp olive oil
1 tbsp lime juice	1 tsp cumin
½ tsp salt	¼ tsp black pepper

Directions:

(1) No matter whether you're using frozen or fresh corn, steam it for 5 minutes in a steam oven. Give it some time to cool. (2) Add the steamed corn, cilantro, red onion, and black beans to a big bowl. (3) The lime juice, cumin, olive oil, salt, and black pepper should be whisked together in a small bowl. (4) Toss the salad to blend after pouring the dressing over it. (5) Enjoy right away, or let it cool in the fridge.

68. Lemon Rosemary Chicken

Total Time: 35 minutes | Prep Time: 10 minutes

Ingredients:

2 boneless, skinless chicken breasts	1 tbsp olive oil
2 tsp fresh rosemary, chopped	1 tsp lemon zest
1 tbsp lemon juice	1 tsp garlic powder
½ tsp salt	½ tsp black pepper

Directions:

(1) Before using, bring the steam oven up to a heat of 190°C. (2) Combine the rosemary, olive oil, zested and juiced lemons, garlic powder, salt, and pepper in a small bowl. (3) Rub the pepper mix on the chicken breasts. After 25 minutes, or when the internal temperature reaches 165°F (75°C), transfer the chicken to a dish that can be used to steam in an oven. (4) After 5 minutes, set aside to cool.

69. Balsamic Roasted Stuffed Peppers

Total Time: 40 minutes | Prep Time: 15 minutes

Ingredients:

2 large bell peppers, halved and seeds removed	½ cup cooked quinoa
½ cup cherry tomatoes, chopped	¼ cup feta cheese, crumbled
1 tbsp balsamic vinegar	1 tbsp olive oil
1 tsp dried oregano	½ tsp salt
¼ tsp black pepper	

Directions:

(1) Before using, bring the steam oven up to a heat of 190°C. (2) Whisk together the quinoa, feta, tomatoes, balsamic vinegar, olive oil, oregano, salt, & pepper in a dish. (3) Spoon the filling into the pepper halves. (4) To make sure the peppers are soft, put the filled peppers on a dish that may be steam-oven-safe and simmer for 25 minutes. (5) Warm before serving.

70. Thai Red Curry Chicken Soup

Total Time: 35 minutes | Prep Time: 10 minutes

Ingredients:

2 cups chicken broth	1 cup coconut milk
1 cup cooked shredded chicken	½ cup red bell pepper, sliced
½ cup carrots, julienned	1 tbsp Thai red curry paste
1 tbsp fish sauce	1 tbsp lime juice
1 tsp fresh ginger, grated	1 tbsp fresh cilantro, chopped

Directions:

(1) A steam oven should be preheated to 375°F, or 190°C. (2) Put the chicken broth, coconut milk, fish sauce, ginger, lime juice, and red curry paste into a saucepan that can withstand steam. (3) Toss in some carrots, bell peppers, and shredded chicken. Mix thoroughly. (4) Ten minutes in the steamer will give the flavors time to meld. (5) Top with chopped cilantro and serve while still hot.

71. Lemon Herb Salmon

Total Time: 20 minutes | Prep Time: 10 minutes

Ingredients:

2 salmon fillets (6 oz each)	1 lemon, sliced
2 tbsp olive oil	2 cloves garlic, minced
1 tsp dried oregano	1 tsp dried thyme

½ tsp salt ½ tsp black pepper

Fresh parsley for garnish

Directions:

(1) Start the steam oven at 212 degrees Fahrenheit (100 degrees Celsius). (2) Steam the salmon fillets on a baking sheet lined with parchment paper. (3) Put the garlic, oregano, thyme, salt, and pepper into a small bowl and stir in the olive oil. (4) Apply the marinade to the salmon fillets using a brush. (5) Place a slice of lemon on top of every fillet. (6) After 10 minutes of steaming, the salmon should flake readily when tested with a fork. (7) Serve immediately after garnishing with fresh parsley.

72. Roasted Garlic Mashed Potatoes

Total Time: 40 minutes | Prep Time: 15 minutes

Ingredients:

4 large russet potatoes, peeled and cubed	1 head of garlic, roasted
½ cup milk	3 tbsp butter
½ tsp salt	½ tsp black pepper
2 tbsp chopped chives (optional)	

Directions:

(1) Start the steam oven at 212 degrees Fahrenheit (100 degrees Celsius). (2) To get fork-tender potatoes, steam the cubed potatoes for 25 minutes in a steam-safe dish. (3) Put the roasted garlic cloves in a basin and mash them while they steam. (4) Mash the cooked potatoes until they are completely smooth. (5) Toss the warmed milk and butter into the mashed potatoes. (6) Add the mashed garlic, salt, & pepper & stir to combine. (7) Top with minced chives and serve while still heated.

73. Lemon Herb Baked Tilapia

Total Time: 18 minutes | Prep Time: 8 minutes

Ingredients:

2 tilapia fillets (6 oz each)	1 lemon, juiced
2 tbsp olive oil	2 cloves garlic, minced
1 tsp dried basil	½ tsp paprika
½ tsp salt	½ tsp black pepper

Directions:

(1) Turn on the steam-bake setting of your steam oven and heat it to 212°F, or 100°C. (2) In a separate small bowl, marge the olive oil, lemon juice, garlic, basil, paprika, salt, and pepper. Whisk to combine. (3) After brushing the tilapia fillets with the spice mixture, set them in a baking dish that can withstand steam. (4) After 10 minutes of steam baking, the fish should be opaque and flake readily when tested with a fork. (5) Top with more lemon wedges and serve right away.

74. Thai Coconut Shrimp

Total Time: 22 minutes | Prep Time: 12 minutes

Ingredients:

1 lb large shrimp, peeled and deveined	1 cup coconut milk
1 tbsp red curry paste	2 cloves garlic, minced
1 tbsp lime juice	1 tbsp soy sauce
½ tsp salt	½ tsp black pepper

2 tbsp chopped cilantro for garnish

Directions:

(1) Start the steam oven at 212 degrees Fahrenheit (100 degrees Celsius). (2) Combine all of the ingredients in a bowl and whisk until smooth. Add garlic, lime juice, soy sauce, salt, and pepper. (3) Pour the coconut mixture over the shrimp in a dish that may be steam-safe. (4) The shrimp should become opaque and pink after 8 minutes of steaming. (5) Serve heated with chopped cilantro as a garnish.

75. Garlic Butter Roasted Carrots

Total Time: 30 minutes | Prep Time: 10 minutes

Ingredients:

1 lb baby carrots	2 tbsp butter, melted
2 cloves garlic, minced	1 tsp honey
½ tsp salt	½ tsp black pepper
1 tbsp chopped parsley for garnish	

Directions:

(1) Set the steam oven to steam-roast mode and heat it up to 375°F, or 190°C. (2) Combine garlic, honey, salt, and pepper with melted butter in a bowl. (3) Gently combine the young carrots with the garlic butter. (4) Evenly distribute the carrots on a baking sheet that can withstand steam. (5) For 20 minutes, steam-roast until soft and slightly browned. (6) Serve heated with a sprinkle of minced parsley for garnish.

76. Lemon Garlic Shrimp and Vegetables

Total Time: 20 minutes | Prep Time: 10 minutes

Ingredients:

1 lb (450g) large shrimp, peeled & deveined	1 zucchini, sliced
1 bell pepper, sliced	1 cup cherry tomatoes, halved
3 cloves garlic, minced	2 tbsp olive oil
1 tbsp lemon juice	1 tsp lemon zest
1/2 tsp salt	1/4 tsp black pepper
1/2 tsp red pepper flakes (optional)	1/2 tsp dried oregano
Fresh parsley, chopped (for garnish)	

Directions:

(1) Bring the steam oven up to temperature, then set it to 212°F or 100°C. (2) Toss together the shrimp, bell pepper, zucchini, garlic, olive oil, lemon zest, lemon juice, salt, pepper, red pepper flakes, & oregano in a bowl. (3) On a steam oven baking sheet, evenly distribute the ingredients. (4) Cook the shrimp in a steamer for 8 to 10 minutes or until they become opaque and pink. (5) When ready to serve, take it out of the oven and top with chopped fresh parsley.

77. Lemon Herb Roasted Veggies

Total Time: 30 minutes | Prep Time: 10 minutes

Ingredients:

1 cup broccoli florets	1 cup cauliflower florets
1 zucchini, sliced	1 red bell pepper, sliced
1 yellow bell pepper, sliced	2 tbsp olive oil
1 tbsp lemon juice	1 tsp lemon zest
1 tsp dried oregano	1/2 tsp dried thyme
1/2 tsp garlic powder	1/2 tsp salt
1/4 tsp black pepper	

Directions:

(1) Turn the steam oven's convection steam setting up to 375°F, or 190°C. (2) Combine the veggies in a big basin and add the olive oil, lemon zest & juice, oregano, thyme, garlic powder, salt, and pepper. Mix well. (3) On a steam oven baking sheet, arrange the veggies in a single layer. (4) To get a somewhat caramelized and soft texture, roast for eighteen to twenty minutes, stirring once halfway through. (5) After taking it out of the oven, you may have it warm as a side dish.

78. Spinach and Ricotta Stuffed Bell Peppers

Total Time: 40 minutes | Prep Time: 15 minutes

Ingredients:

4 large bell peppers, halved and seeds removed	2 cups fresh spinach, chopped
1 cup ricotta cheese	1/2 cup grated Parmesan cheese
1/2 cup cooked quinoa or rice	1 clove garlic, minced
1/2 tsp salt	1/4 tsp black pepper
1/2 tsp dried basil	1/4 tsp red pepper flakes (optional)

Directions:

(1) Bring the steam oven up to temperature, then set it to 212°F or 100°C. (2) Add the quinoa, garlic, ricotta, Parmesan, basil, salt, pepper, & red pepper flakes to a bowl with the spinach and mix well. (3) Divide the filling among the bell pepper halves & place them on a skillet to steam in the oven. Give the peppers a quarter of an hour in the steamer to soften. (4) Take it out of the oven and enjoy it hot.

79. Moroccan Chicken Tagine

Total Time: 50 minutes | Prep Time: 15 minutes

Ingredients:

4 boneless, skinless chicken thighs	1 small onion, finely chopped
2 cloves garlic, minced	1 cup diced tomatoes
1/2 cup chicken broth	1/2 cup chickpeas, drained
1/2 cup sliced carrots	1/2 cup sliced zucchini
1/4 cup raisins	1 tsp ground cumin
1 tsp ground coriander	1/2 tsp ground cinnamon
1/2 tsp smoked paprika	1/2 tsp salt
1/4 tsp black pepper	1 tbsp olive oil
Fresh cilantro, chopped (for garnish)	

Directions:

(1) Turn the steam oven's temperature up to 212 degrees Fahrenheit (100 degrees Celsius). (2) Toss together the following ingredients in a steam oven dish: chicken thighs, garlic, onion, tomatoes, chicken broth, chickpeas, carrots, zucchini, raisins, cinnamon, cumin, coriander, paprika, salt, pepper, to taste, and olive oil. (3) Submerge in steam for 40 minutes, tossing halfway through, with a lid or foil covering. (4) Take it out of the oven, top it with chopped cilantro, & serve it over rice or couscous.

80. Spinach & Feta Stuffed Chicken Breasts

Total Time: 35 minutes | Prep Time: 10 minutes

Ingredients:

2 large boneless, skinless chicken breasts	1 cup fresh spinach, chopped
1/2 cup crumbled feta cheese	1 clove garlic, minced
1/2 tsp dried oregano	1/4 tsp salt
1/4 tsp black pepper	1 tbsp olive oil

Directions:

(1) Turn the steam oven's convection steam setting up to 350°F, or 175°C. (2) Make a shallow incision in the center of each chicken breast; do not cut through. (3) Garlic, oregano, salt, pepper, feta cheese, spinach, and a little bowl should do it. (4) Fill up the chicken breasts with the filling and, if needed, use toothpicks to keep them in place. (5) Olive oil the chicken breasts and set them on a steam oven pan. (6) Put it in the steamer for 25 minutes, or until the temperature inside hits 165°F, which is 75°C. (7) Take it out of the oven and let it sit for 5 minutes before cutting into it.

81. Roasted Vegetable Lasagna

Total Time: 1 hour 15 minutes | Prep Time: 25 minutes | Cook Time: 50 minutes

Ingredients:

1 zucchini, sliced	1 red bell pepper, sliced
1 yellow bell pepper, sliced	1 eggplant, sliced
2 cups spinach, chopped	1 ½ cups ricotta cheese
1 ½ cups mozzarella cheese, shredded	½ cup Parmesan cheese, grated
1 jar (24 oz) marinara sauce	12 lasagna sheets, no-boil
2 tablespoons olive oil	1 teaspoon Italian seasoning
½ teaspoon salt	½ teaspoon black pepper

Directions:

(1) Bring the steam oven up to temperature (350°F, 180°C) and add 30% steam. (2) In a large bowl, marinate the eggplant, bell peppers, zucchini, salt, pepper, and Italian seasoning. Toss to coat. After 15 minutes in the oven, transfer to a baking sheet. (3) Ricotta cheese and spinach should be combined in a bowl. (4) Layer marinara sauce in a baking dish. After that, layer lasagna sheets. Then, top with roasted veggies. Finally, top with ricotta mixture and mozzarella. Layer again, this time topping with mozzarella and marinara. (5) Bake for 35 minutes with the foil on top. Ten more minutes of exposed baking after removing foil; top with Parmesan. (6) Ten minutes should pass before slicing.

82. Stuffed Zucchini with Sausage

Total Time: 50 minutes | Prep Time: 15 minutes | Cook Time: 35 minutes

Ingredients:

- 4 medium zucchinis, halved lengthwise
- ½ cup onion, finely chopped
- 1 cup cherry tomatoes, chopped
- ¼ cup Parmesan cheese, grated
- ½ teaspoon salt
- ½ pound Italian sausage, crumbled
- 1 garlic clove, minced
- ½ cup mozzarella cheese, shredded
- ½ teaspoon dried oregano
- ¼ teaspoon black pepper

Directions:

(1) Turn on the steam oven to 350°F (180°C) and add 50% steam. (2) Extract the zucchini flesh, being sure to leave a border of half an inch. Before setting aside, mince the meat. (3) Sardines should be fried in a pan set over medium heat. Chopped zucchini flesh, onion, and garlic should be added. Sauté for three minutes. (4) Add the oregano, cherry tomatoes, salt, and pepper and stir to combine. Add two more minutes of cooking time. (5) Spoon sausage mixture into zucchini halves; sprinkle mozzarella and Parmesan on top. (6) After 25 minutes in a steam oven, the zucchini should be soft, and the cheese should be bubbling.

83. Spinach and Ricotta Stuffed Eggplant

Total Time: 55 minutes | Prep Time: 20 minutes | Cook Time: 35 minutes

Ingredients:

- 2 large eggplants, halved
- 1 cup ricotta cheese
- 1 cup fresh spinach, chopped
- ½ teaspoon garlic powder
- ¼ teaspoon black pepper
- ½ cup mozzarella cheese, shredded
- ¼ cup Parmesan cheese, grated
- ½ teaspoon salt
- 1 cup marinara sauce

Directions:

(1) Gather 50% steam and heat the steam oven to 375°F, or 190°C. (2) Leave a ½-inch shell after scooping out some eggplant flesh. Break the meat into small pieces. (3) Add the ricotta, spinach, eggplant, Parmesan, garlic powder, salt, & pepper to a bowl & stir to combine. (4) After stuffing the eggplants, sprinkle with mozzarella and marinara sauce. (5) Bake, covered with a steam oven tray, for 35 minutes or until soft & lightly browned.

84. Thai Red Curry Chicken and Vegetables

Total Time: 45 minutes | Prep Time: 15 minutes | Cook Time: 30 minutes

Ingredients:

- 2 boneless, skinless chicken breasts, cubed
- 1 zucchini, sliced
- 1 can (14 oz) coconut milk
- 1 tablespoon fish sauce
- 1 teaspoon ginger, grated
- 1 tablespoon olive oil
- 1 red bell pepper, sliced
- 1 cup broccoli florets
- 2 tablespoons Thai red curry paste
- 1 tablespoon soy sauce
- 2 garlic cloves, minced
- ½ teaspoon salt

½ teaspoon black pepper

Directions:

(1) Gather 50% steam and heat the steam oven to 375°F, or 190°C. (2) Combine the red curry paste, coconut milk, fish sauce, soy sauce, ginger, & garlic in a bowl and whisk to combine. (3) In a dish that can be steamed in an oven, mix together the chicken, bell pepper, zucchini, and broccoli. Sprinkle with pepper, salt, and olive oil. (4) Add the curry sauce & stir to combine. (5) Stir once throughout the 30 minutes of baking. Top with steaming rice and serve hot.

85. Spinach and Feta Stuffed Chicken

Total Time: 45 minutes | Prep Time: 15 minutes | Cook Time: 30 minutes

Ingredients:

2 large boneless, skinless chicken breasts	1 cup fresh spinach, chopped
½ cup feta cheese, crumbled	½ teaspoon garlic powder
½ teaspoon dried oregano	½ teaspoon salt
¼ teaspoon black pepper	1 tablespoon olive oil

Directions:

(1) Get the steam oven up to temperature (375°F/190°C) using 40% steam. (2) Divide the chicken breasts in half lengthwise. (3) Combine spinach, feta, oregano, salt, and pepper in a bowl. Add garlic powder and stir. (4) After stuffing the chicken pockets, use toothpicks to keep the filling in place. (5) Before placing it on a dish that may be steam-oven-safe, brush it with olive oil. (6) Bake for 30 minutes or un till a thermometer reads 74°C when tested in the center.

86. Spinach Artichoke Stuffed Chicken

Total Time: 40 minutes | Prep Time: 15 minutes | Cook Time: 25 minutes

Ingredients:

4 boneless, skinless chicken breasts	1 cup fresh spinach, chopped
½ cup canned artichoke hearts, chopped	½ cup cream cheese, softened
¼ cup grated Parmesan cheese	1 teaspoon garlic powder
1 teaspoon onion powder	½ teaspoon salt
½ teaspoon black pepper	1 tablespoon olive oil

Directions:

(1) Get the steam oven up to temperature (200°C or 400°F) and add 30% steam. (2) In a bowl, marge the artichoke hearts, spinach, cream cheese, Parmesan, garlic powder, onion powder, salt, and black pepper. Spread out the ingredients. Stuff the chicken breasts by cutting a pocket into each one. (3) After brushing the chicken with olive oil, set it on a baking dish and put it in the steam oven. (4) After 25 minutes of steam roasting, the chicken should be cooked through, with an internal temperature of 75°C. (5) Allow to cool for five minutes before consumption.

87. Lemon Garlic Herb Roasted Carrots

Total Time: 30 minutes | Prep Time: 10 minutes | Cook Time: 20 minutes

Ingredients:

1 pound carrots, peeled & cut into sticks	2 tablespoons olive oil
2 cloves garlic, minced	1 tablespoon lemon juice
1 teaspoon dried thyme	½ teaspoon salt
½ teaspoon black pepper	

Directions:

(1) Steam the oven to 200°C (400°F) with half of the steam turned on. (2) Marinate the carrots in a mixture of garlic, lemon juice, thyme, salt, and pepper. Toss to coat. (3) Arrange the carrots in a single layer on a steam oven pan. (4) Cook, stirring once, for 20 minutes or until soft and browned. (5) Warm it up and put it on the side.

88. Thai Peanut Chicken Skewers

Total Time: 35 minutes | Prep Time: 15 minutes | Cook Time: 20 minutes

Ingredients:

2 chicken breasts (without bones & skin) diced into 1-inch pieces	¼ cup peanut butter
2 tablespoons soy sauce	1 tablespoon honey
1 tablespoon lime juice	1 teaspoon grated ginger
2 cloves garlic, minced	½ teaspoon chili flakes
Wooden skewers that have been immersed in water for half an hour	

Directions:

(1) With 30% steam, bring the steam oven up to a temperature of 375°F. (2) Blend together peanut butter, honey, soy sauce, lime juice, ginger, garlic, & chili flakes in a bowl. (3) Marinate the chicken cubes for 10 minutes after tossing them in the sauce. (4) Arrange the chicken on a steam oven tray after threading it onto skewers. (5) Turn the chicken over halfway through cooking time to ensure even browning and complete cooking. Cook for 20 minutes. (6) To dip, serve with more peanut sauce.

89. Roasted Cauliflower with Garlic and Herbs

Total Time: 30 minutes | Prep Time: 10 minutes | Cook Time: 20 minutes

Ingredients:

1 medium head cauliflower, cut into florets	2 tablespoons olive oil
3 cloves garlic, minced	1 teaspoon dried oregano
1 teaspoon dried thyme	½ teaspoon salt
½ teaspoon black pepper	¼ teaspoon red pepper flakes (optional)

Directions:

(1) 200°C (400°F) of steam is required to get the steam oven up to temperature. (2) Sprinkle the florets of cauliflower with salt, pepper, oregano, thyme, olive oil, and garlic. (3) Arrange evenly on a steam oven baking sheet. (4) To get a golden brown and soft texture, roast for 20 minutes while tossing halfway through. (5) As a garnish, you may add red pepper flakes and serve warm.

90. Thai Green Curry Vegetables

Total Time: 35 minutes | Prep Time: 15 minutes | Cook Time: 20 minutes

Ingredients:

1 cup broccoli florets	1 cup bell peppers, sliced
1 cup zucchini, sliced	1 small carrot, julienned
1 cup coconut milk	2 tablespoons Thai green curry paste
1 teaspoon soy sauce	½ teaspoon brown sugar
1 tablespoon lime juice	1 tablespoon fresh basil leaves

Directions:

(1) With 40% steam, bring the steam oven up to a temperature of 375°F. (2) Combine the green curry paste, lime juice, brown sugar, coconut milk, and soy sauce in a bowl and whisk to combine. (3) Pour the curry sauce over the veggies in a dish that may be steam-oven-safe. (4) After 20 minutes of steaming, the veggies should be soft but still have some color. (5) Serve over steaming rice and top with fresh basil.

91. Apple Cinnamon Pork Chops

Total Time: 30 minutes | Prep Time: 10 minutes

Ingredients:

4 boneless pork chops	2 apples, cored and sliced
1 teaspoon cinnamon	1 tablespoon brown sugar
½ teaspoon salt	½ teaspoon black pepper
1 tablespoon olive oil	½ cup apple cider or juice

Directions:

(1) Set the steam oven to a preheated temperature of 375°F, or 190°C, using combination steam. (2) Sprinkle salt, pepper, and olive oil on pork chops. (3) Slice some apples and toss them with some brown sugar and cinnamon in a basin. (4) Spread the apple mixture over the pork chops in a shallow baking dish. Shake in the apple cider. (5) If you want your pork to be perfectly cooked, give it 20 minutes in a steam oven at 145 degrees Fahrenheit (63 degrees Celsius). (6) Wait 5 minutes before cutting and serving.

92. Thai Peanut Chicken Stir-Fry

Total Time: 25 minutes | Prep Time: 10 minutes

Ingredients:

2 boneless, skinless chicken breasts, sliced	1 cup broccoli florets
1 red bell pepper, sliced	1 carrot, julienned
2 tablespoons soy sauce	2 tablespoons peanut butter
1 teaspoon sesame oil	1 teaspoon garlic, minced
½ teaspoon ginger, grated	½ cup chicken broth

Directions:

(1) Set the steam oven to combination steam and heat it to 200°C. (2) Combine peanut butter, chicken broth, sesame oil, garlic, and soy sauce in a bowl. (3) In one steaming tray

with holes, arrange the chicken pieces; in another, arrange the veggies. (4) Ten minutes in the steamer, the chicken and veggies will be cooked. (5) Before putting the chicken and vegetables back in the oven for five more minutes, toss them with the peanut sauce. (6) Top with steaming rice and serve hot.

93. Spaghetti Carbonara

Total Time: 20 minutes | Prep Time: 10 minutes

Ingredients:

- 12 oz spaghetti
- 4 oz pancetta, diced
- 2 large eggs
- ½ cup Parmesan cheese, grated
- ½ teaspoon black pepper
- 1 clove garlic, minced
- 1 tablespoon olive oil

Directions:

(1) On steam mode, bring the steam oven up to 212°F, or 100°C. (2) Cover the spaghetti with water in a steam-safe dish. Bring to a boil & cook for ten minutes or until the bite is just right. Run off. (3) Get the pancetta crispy while the pasta is cooking. For a further minute, sauté the garlic. (4) Crack eggs into a bowl & whisk in the Parmesan and black pepper. (5) To make a creamy sauce, immediately toss together the pancetta, egg mixture, and heated pasta. (6) Top with more Parmesan and serve right away.

94. Roasted Cauliflower Steaks

Total Time: 35 minutes | Prep Time: 10 minutes

Ingredients:

- 1 large cauliflower, cut into 1-inch steaks
- 2 tablespoons olive oil
- 1 teaspoon garlic powder
- ½ teaspoon smoked paprika
- ½ teaspoon salt
- ¼ teaspoon black pepper
- ½ cup grated Parmesan cheese (optional)

Directions:

(1) Set the steam oven to combination steam and heat it to 200°C. (2) Olive oil, garlic powder, paprika, salt, and pepper should be brushed over cauliflower steaks before cooking. (3) Place in the oven & cook for 20 minutes, turning once. (4) Roast for a further 10 minutes, or until steaks are brown, then sprinkle with Parmesan, if using. (5) Keep heated before serving.

95. Lemon Herb Stuffed Mushrooms

Total Time: 25 minutes | Prep Time: 10 minutes

Ingredients:

- 12 large mushrooms, stems removed
- ½ cup breadcrumbs
- ¼ cup Parmesan cheese, grated
- 2 tablespoons fresh parsley, chopped
- 1 clove garlic, minced
- 1 tablespoon lemon juice
- 1 teaspoon olive oil
- ½ teaspoon salt
- ¼ teaspoon black pepper

Directions:

(1) Switch to combined steam mode and heat the steam oven to 375°F, or 190°C. (2) Combine breadcrumbs, Parmesan, herb, garlic, lemon zest, olive oil, salt, & pepper in a mixing

bowl. (3) Fill the mushroom caps with the filling. (4) Steam roast, uncovered, for 15 minutes or until a golden brown color appears. (5) Keep heated before serving.

96. Sweet Potato and Black Bean Chili

Total Time: 40 minutes | Prep Time: 15 minutes

Ingredients:

2 medium sweet potatoes, peeled and diced	1 can black beans, drained & rinsed
1 can diced tomatoes	1 cup vegetable broth
1 small onion, chopped	2 cloves garlic, minced
1 tsp cumin	1 tsp smoked paprika
½ tsp chili powder	½ tsp salt
¼ tsp black pepper	1 tbsp olive oil
1 tbsp lime juice	Fresh cilantro for garnish

Directions:

(1) The steam oven has to be preheated to 210°F, or 100°C, with 100% steam. (2) Sauté the garlic & onions in olive oil until they release their aroma in a skillet that can withstand steam. (3) Season with salt, pepper, cumin, paprika, black beans, chopped tomatoes, broth, and sweet potatoes. Mix thoroughly. (4) Steam the sweet potatoes for 25 minutes with the foil on top or until they are soft. (5) After you've adjusted the spice, stir in the lime juice and serve with cilantro as a garnish.

97. Asian-Style Salmon

Total Time: 25 minutes | Prep Time: 10 minutes

Ingredients:

2 salmon fillets	2 tbsp low-sodium soy sauce
1 tbsp honey	1 tsp sesame oil
1 tsp grated ginger	1 clove garlic, minced
½ tsp chili flakes (optional)	1 tbsp green onions, chopped
1 tsp sesame seeds	

Directions:

(1) A steam oven preheated to 100% steam should reach a temperature of 200°F, or 93°C. (2) In a separate small bowl, marge the soy sauce, honey, sesame oil, ginger, garlic, and chili flakes. Whisk to combine. (3) Cover the salmon fillets with marinade and set them in a dish that can be steam-cooked. (4) Once the salmon flakes easily, it's done cooking; steam it for 15 minutes. (5) Sprinkle some sesame seeds & green onions on top before you serve.

98. Greek Stuffed Zucchini Boats

Total Time: 35 minutes | Prep Time: 15 minutes

Ingredients:

2 large zucchinis, halved lengthwise	½ lb ground turkey or beef
1 small onion, diced	1 clove garlic, minced
½ cup cooked quinoa	½ cup diced tomatoes
¼ cup crumbled feta cheese	1 tsp dried oregano
½ tsp salt	¼ tsp black pepper
1 tbsp olive oil	

Directions:

(1) The steam oven has to be preheated to 210°F, or 100°C, with 100% steam. (2) Remove the pulp from the zucchini and use it to make boats. (3) While the olive oil is heating, sauté the garlic and onion. Cook the ground beef until it becomes brown. (4) Chop the tomatoes and add them to the quinoa along with the pulp, oregano, salt, and pepper. Allow to cook for a duration of 5 minutes. (5) Top with feta cheese and stuff zucchini halves with the mixture. (6) To make them soft, steam them for 20 minutes in a steam-safe dish.

99. Mediterranean Roasted Chicken

Total Time: 45 minutes | Prep Time: 15 minutes

Ingredients:

4 bone-in, skin-on chicken thighs	1 lemon, sliced
½ cup cherry tomatoes, halved	½ cup Kalamata olives, pitted
2 tbsp olive oil	1 tsp dried oregano
½ tsp paprika	½ tsp garlic powder
½ tsp salt	¼ tsp black pepper

Directions:

(1) Bring the steam oven up to temperature using a mixture of steam and convection, around 60% steam and 40% heat. (2) Garlic powder, oregano, paprika, olive oil, salt, and pepper should be applied to the chicken. (3) Roast the chicken in a pan that can withstand steam. Set it on a bed of cherry tomatoes, olives, and slices of lemon. (4) Once the internal temperature reaches 75°C and the skin becomes golden, roast for another 30 minutes. (5) Allow to cool for five minutes before consumption.

100. Creamy Avocado Chicken Pasta

Total Time: 30 minutes | Prep Time: 10 minutes

Ingredients:

8 oz whole wheat pasta	2 boneless, skinless chicken breasts, cubed
1 ripe avocado	½ cup plain Greek yogurt
1 clove garlic, minced	½ lemon, juiced
1 tbsp olive oil	½ tsp salt
¼ tsp black pepper	¼ tsp red pepper flakes (optional)
¼ cup grated Parmesan cheese	Fresh basil for garnish

Directions:

(1) The steam oven has to be preheated to 212°F, or 100°C, with 100% steam. (2) Ten minutes of steaming in a skillet with holes in it will get pasta al dente. Reserve the drained liquid. (3) Cook the chicken thoroughly by steaming it for 12–15 minutes in a separate pan. (4) Toss the avocado, yogurt, garlic, lemon juice, olive oil, salt, and pepper in a blender. Puree the mixture. (5) Combine the chicken, avocado sauce, and spaghetti. (6) Prior to serving, top with fresh basil, Parmesan, and red pepper flakes.

101. Creamy Spinach and Ricotta Stuffed Shells

Total Time: 45 minutes | Prep Time: 15 minutes | Cook Time: 30 minutes

Ingredients:

12 jumbo pasta shells	1 cup ricotta cheese
½ cup grated Parmesan cheese	1 cup shredded mozzarella cheese
1 cup fresh spinach, chopped	1 egg
1 teaspoon garlic powder	½ teaspoon salt
½ teaspoon black pepper	1½ cups marinara sauce

Directions:

(1) Furnish the steam oven with a 50% combination steam setting and heat it to 375°F (190°C). (2) Boil water and cook shells of pasta until they are just barely done. Reserve the drained liquid. (3) Toss together the ricotta, mozzarella, Parmesan, spinach, egg, garlic powder, salt, and pepper in a combined bowl. (4) Before placing the shells in the oven, fill them with the ricotta mixture. (5) Spoon the shells with marinara sauce. (6) To make sure it's hot and bubbling, steam-bake it for 25 to 30 minutes. (7) Allow it to cool for a moment before you eat.

102. Mediterranean Chickpea and Vegetable Salad

Total Time: 25 minutes | Prep Time: 15 minutes | Cook Time: 10 minutes

Ingredients:

1 cup canned chickpeas, drained and rinsed	1 cup cherry tomatoes, halved
½ cup cucumber, diced	½ cup red bell pepper, diced
¼ cup red onion, finely chopped	¼ cup Kalamata olives, sliced
¼ cup feta cheese, crumbled	2 tablespoons olive oil
1 tablespoon lemon juice	1 teaspoon dried oregano
Salt and black pepper to taste	

Directions:

(1) Make sure the steam oven is set to full steam and heated to 212°F (100°C). (2) Simmer the chickpeas for 10 minutes in a steamer with holes in it until they are tender. (3) Add the chickpeas, cherry tomatoes, cucumber, bell pepper, onion, and olives to a bowl and mix well. (4) Olive oil, lemon juice, oregano, salt, and pepper should be drizzled over the top. (5) Add the feta cheese & toss to combine.

103. Roasted Stuffed Bell Peppers

Total Time: 50 minutes | Prep Time: 15 minutes | Cook Time: 35 minutes

Ingredients:

4 large bell peppers (red, yellow, or green)	1 cup cooked quinoa
½ cup black beans drained and rinsed	½ cup corn kernels
½ cup diced tomatoes	¼ cup chopped fresh cilantro
1 teaspoon cumin	½ teaspoon chili powder
½ teaspoon salt	½ teaspoon black pepper
½ cup shredded cheese (cheddar or Monterey Jack)	

Directions:

(1) Bring the temperature of the steam oven up to 190°C, & set the combined steam level to 50%. (2) First, you'll need to trim the bell peppers and take out their seeds. (3) Cobble together the quinoa, black beans, corn, tomatoes, cilantro, cumin, chili powder, salt, & pepper in a bowl. (4) Seal the peppers and stuff them with the mixture. Bake them. (5) On top, crumble some cheese. (6) Melt the cheese and steam-bake the peppers for 30–35 minutes or until they are soft. (7) Serve after letting it cool for a short while.

104. Lemon Garlic Roasted Veggies

Total Time: 30 minutes | Prep Time: 10 minutes | Cook Time: 20 minutes

Ingredients:

1 zucchini, sliced	1 yellow squash, sliced
1 red bell pepper, chopped	1 cup broccoli florets
1 cup cauliflower florets	2 tablespoons olive oil
2 cloves garlic, minced	1 tablespoon lemon juice
1 teaspoon dried thyme	Salt and black pepper to taste

Directions:

(1) Bring the steam oven up to temperature (400°F or 200°C) and set the combined steam to 50%. (2) Add the garlic, olive oil, lemon juice, thyme, salt, & pepper to a bowl & mix in the veggies. (3) On a baking sheet, distribute the veggies in an equal layer. (4) Cook in a steam oven for about 18 to 20 minutes or until soft and just slightly browned. (5) Warm it up and put it on the side.

105. Thai Basil Chicken Stir-Fry

Total Time: 25 minutes | Prep Time: 10 minutes | Cook Time: 15 minutes

Ingredients:

1 pound boneless, skinless chicken thighs, sliced	1 tablespoon vegetable oil
2 cloves garlic, minced	1 red chili, sliced (optional)
2 tablespoons soy sauce	1 tablespoon oyster sauce
1 teaspoon fish sauce	1 teaspoon sugar
1 cup fresh Thai basil leaves	1 cup steamed jasmine rice (for serving)

Directions:

(1) The steam oven should be preheated to 212°F, or 100°C, on the full-steam setting. (2) Cook the chicken in a steamer for 10 minutes or until it is almost done. (3) Saute the garlic and chili in heated oil till they release their aroma. (4) After 3–4 minutes, stir in the steamed chicken. (5) Toss in the sugar, fish sauce, oyster sauce, and soy sauce. (6) Cook for one further minute or until the Thai basil leaves wilt, then add them. (7) Top with hot jasmine rice that has been cooked.

106. Thai Chicken Skewers

Total Time: 35 minutes | Prep Time: 15 minutes | Cook Time: 20 minutes

Ingredients:

1-pound strip-filet of skinless, boneless chicken breast	2 tbsp soy sauce
1 tbsp fish sauce	1 tbsp honey

1 tbsp lime juice	1 tbsp sesame oil
1 tsp grated ginger	2 cloves garlic, minced
½ tsp red pepper flakes	Wooden or metal skewers

Directions:

(1) A steam oven preheated to 50% steam may reach temperatures of 190°C (375°F). (2) Combine all of the ingredients in a bowl and whisk until smooth. Add the lime juice, ginger, garlic, honey, fish sauce, sesame oil, and red pepper flakes. (3) After coating the chicken strips, add them to the marinade. Wait 10 minutes before serving. (4) After threading the chicken onto skewers, set it on a parchment paper-lined, perforated tray. (5) To cook the chicken thoroughly, steam roast it for eighteen to twenty minutes, flipping once halfway through. (6) Sauces like peanut or Thai sweet chili are perfect for topping off a side dish.

107. Greek Lemon Chicken Soup (Avgolemono)

Total Time: 30 minutes | Prep Time: 10 minutes | Cook Time: 20 minutes

Ingredients:

4 cups chicken broth	½ cup orzo pasta
2 cups cooked, shredded chicken	2 large eggs
Juice of 2 lemons	1 tsp salt
½ tsp black pepper	1 tbsp chopped fresh dill

Directions:

(1) Turn the steam oven on high heat and get it up to 212 degrees Fahrenheit (100 degrees Celsius). (2) Combine the orzo pasta and chicken stock in a basin that can be steam-safe. Gently boil for ten minutes. (3) In another dish, whisk together the eggs and lemon juice. Add a ladleful of boiling broth slowly while whisking continuously. (4) Reintroduce the egg mixture and shredded chicken to the soup. Continue steaming for a further five minutes. (5) Put some salt, pepper, and dill on top. Keep heated before serving.

108. Spicy Garlic Shrimp

Total Time: 20 minutes | Prep Time: 10 minutes | Cook Time: 10 minutes

Ingredients:

1 lb large shrimp, peeled and deveined	3 cloves garlic, minced
1 tbsp olive oil	1 tbsp soy sauce
1 tsp red pepper flakes	½ tsp smoked paprika
½ tsp salt	¼ tsp black pepper
Juice of 1 lemon	1 tbsp chopped parsley

Directions:

(1) Get the steam oven up to temperature (400°F or 200°C) and add 30% steam. (2) Combine the shrimp with the red pepper flakes, olive oil, soy sauce, garlic, salt, and pepper in a bowl. (3) Spread the shrimp out evenly on a tray with holes punched into it. (4) Cook the shrimp in a steam oven for 8 to 10 minutes or until they become opaque and curl. (5) Before serving, drizzle with lemon juice and top with parsley.

109. Creamy Tomato Basil Chicken

Total Time: 35 minutes | Prep Time: 15 minutes | Cook Time: 20 minutes

Ingredients:

2 boneless, skinless chicken breasts	1 cup cherry tomatoes, halved

- ½ cup heavy cream
- ¼ cup grated Parmesan cheese
- 2 cloves garlic, minced
- 1 tbsp olive oil
- 1 tsp dried oregano
- ½ tsp salt
- ¼ tsp black pepper
- ¼ cup fresh basil, chopped

Directions:

(1) Gather 50% steam and heat the steam oven to 375°F, or 190°C. (2) Toss the chicken with the oregano, pepper, and salt. Once prepared, transfer to a baking dish that can withstand steam. (3) After a couple of minutes of sautéing garlic in olive oil, toss in the cherry tomatoes. (4) Add the Parmesan & heavy cream and stir to combine. The sauce should be poured over the chicken once it has been mixed. (5) To ensure the chicken is done all the way through, steam roast it for 20 minutes. (6) Add some fresh basil as a garnish just before serving.

110. Spinach and Feta Stuffed Peppers

Total Time: 40 minutes | Prep Time: 15 minutes | Cook Time: 25 minutes

Ingredients:

- 4 large bell peppers, halved and deseeded
- 2 cups fresh spinach, chopped
- 1 cup cooked quinoa
- ½ cup crumbled feta cheese
- ¼ cup chopped sun-dried tomatoes
- 2 cloves garlic, minced
- 1 tbsp olive oil
- ½ tsp dried oregano
- ½ tsp salt
- ¼ tsp black pepper

Directions:

(1) Heat 60% steam in a steam oven until it reaches 350°F or 175°C. (2) Before adding the spinach, sauté the garlic in olive oil in a pan until the spinach wilts. (3) Stir together the quinoa, feta, sun-dried tomatoes, oregano, salt, and pepper in a mixing bowl. Saute the spinach and stir in. (4) Put half of the mixture into each bell pepper and bake. (5) Peel and soften peppers by steam-roasting them for 25 minutes. Warm before serving.

111. Mediterranean Chicken Bake

Total Time: 40 minutes | Prep Time: 15 minutes | Cook Time: 25 minutes

Ingredients:

- 4 boneless, skinless chicken breasts
- 1 cup cherry tomatoes, halved
- ½ cup kalamata olives, pitted and sliced
- ¼ cup red onion, thinly sliced
- 2 cloves garlic, minced
- 1 teaspoon dried oregano
- ½ teaspoon salt
- ½ teaspoon black pepper
- 2 tablespoons olive oil
- ¼ cup crumbled feta cheese
- 1 tablespoon fresh parsley, chopped
- 1 lemon, cut into wedges

Directions:

(1) Set the steam oven to combined steam and heat it to 375°F, or 190°C. (2) Before baking, coat the chicken breasts with olive oil. (3) Oregano, salt, and black pepper are the seasonings to season. (4) After the chicken is cooked, top it with olives, garlic, red onion, and cherry tomatoes. (5) Place the foil over the pan and steam it for 20 minutes. (6) Remove the lid, top with feta, and continue steaming for five more minutes. (7) Add some fresh parsley as a garnish and serve with lemon wedges.

112. Teriyaki Glazed Carrots

Total Time: 25 minutes | Prep Time: 10 minutes | Cook Time: 15 minutes

Ingredients:

- 1 lb baby carrots
- 2 tablespoons soy sauce
- 1 tablespoon honey
- 1 teaspoon grated ginger
- 1 teaspoon sesame oil
- ½ teaspoon garlic powder
- ½ teaspoon black pepper
- 1 teaspoon sesame seeds (for garnish)
- 1 tablespoon chopped green onions

Directions:

(1) Ready the steam oven for use by setting it to pure steam at 210°F or 100°C. (2) Arrange the carrots in a pan that can withstand steam. (3) Combine the ginger, honey, sesame oil, garlic powder, and black pepper in a small bowl and whisk to combine. (4) Toss the carrots in the dressing after pouring it over them. (5) Cook in a steamer for 15 minutes, whisking occasionally. (6) After taking it out of the oven, top with green onions and sesame seeds.

113. Sesame Ginger Pork

Total Time: 40 minutes | Prep Time: 15 minutes | Cook Time: 25 minutes

Ingredients:

- 1 lb pork tenderloin
- 2 tablespoons soy sauce
- 1 tablespoon honey
- 1 teaspoon grated fresh ginger
- 1 teaspoon sesame oil
- 1 clove garlic, minced
- ½ teaspoon black pepper
- 1 teaspoon sesame seeds (for garnish)
- 2 green onions, sliced

Directions:

(1) Get the steam oven up to temperature, using the combined steam setting, at 350°F (175°C). (2) To make the sauce, combine the honey, ginger, sesame oil, garlic, & black pepper in a small receptacle. (3) Allow the pork tenderloin to sit for 10 minutes after coating it with the marinade. (4) After preparing the baking dish, steam the pork for 20 minutes. (5) For a crust that's caramelized, bump up the temperature to 400°F (200°C) and steam for another 5 minutes. (6) The pork should be rested for 5 minutes before slicing and being garnished with green onions and sesame seeds.

114. Garlic Parmesan Roasted Chicken

Total Time: 50 minutes | Prep Time: 15 minutes | Cook Time: 35 minutes

Ingredients:

- 4 bone-in, skin-on chicken thighs
- 2 tablespoons olive oil
- 3 cloves garlic, minced
- ½ teaspoon salt
- ½ teaspoon black pepper
- 1 teaspoon dried Italian seasoning
- ¼ cup grated Parmesan cheese
- 1 tablespoon fresh parsley, chopped

Directions:

(1) Set the steam oven to combined steam and heat it to 375°F, or 190°C. (2) Combine garlic, olive oil, salt, pepper, and Italian seasoning in a

small bowl. (3) Apply the blend to the thigh meat. (4) After 30 minutes of steaming, transfer the chicken to a baking tray. (5) Coat the chicken with Parmesan and continue steaming for an additional 5 minutes or until it becomes a golden brown color. (6) Put some parsley over the top and serve.

115. Lemon Garlic Tilapia

Total Time: 20 minutes | Prep Time: 10 minutes | Cook Time: 10 minutes

Ingredients:

2 tilapia fillets	1 tablespoon olive oil
2 cloves garlic, minced	½ teaspoon salt
½ teaspoon black pepper	1 lemon, sliced
1 teaspoon fresh parsley, chopped	

Directions:

(1) Ready the steam oven for use by setting it to pure steam at 210°F or 100°C. (2) Get a dish that can withstand steam and add the tilapia fillets. (3) Olive oil, garlic, salt, and pepper should be drizzled over the top. (4) Top with slices of lemon. (5) To get flaky, fully cooked fish, steam for 10 minutes. (6) Sprinkle with chopped fresh parsley before serving.

116. Tomato Basil Soup

Total Time: 35 minutes | Prep Time: 10 minutes

Ingredients:

6 large tomatoes, quartered	1 small onion, chopped
3 cloves garlic, minced	2 cups vegetable broth
½ cup fresh basil leaves	1 tbsp olive oil
1 tsp salt	1/2 tsp black pepper
1/2 cup heavy cream (optional)	

Directions:

(1) On steam mode, bring the steam oven up to 212°F, or 100°C. (2) Arrange the garlic, onion, and tomatoes in a baking dish. Sprinkle with pepper, salt, and olive oil. (3) To get the tomatoes soft, steam them for 20 minutes. (4) Combine all ingredients in a blender and drizzle in the veggie broth. Puree the mixture. (5) Add the basil & simmer for 5 minutes over low heat after pouring into a saucepan. (6) If you want it with additional creaminess, heavy cream is one option. Keep heated before serving.

117. Greek Meatballs

Total Time: 30 minutes | Prep Time: 15 minutes

Ingredients:

1 lb ground lamb (or beef)	1/2 cup breadcrumbs
1 egg	1/4 cup red onion, finely chopped
2 cloves garlic, minced	1 tsp dried oregano
1/2 tsp cumin	1/2 tsp salt
1/4 tsp black pepper	1/4 cup feta cheese, crumbled
1 tbsp olive oil	

Directions:

(1) Turn the steam oven's combined steam and convection feature on high heat until it reaches 350°F or 175°C. (2) Incorporate all of the ingredients in a bowl and stir to incorporate. (3) Roll into little meatballs and set on a parchment-lined, perforated baking sheet. (4)

After 15 minutes of steaming, brown the food by switching to convection mode and cooking it at 400°F (200°C) for five more minutes. (5) Accompany with pita bread and tzatziki sauce.

118. Balsamic Glazed Roasted Chickpeas

Total Time: 25 minutes | Prep Time: 5 minutes

Ingredients:

- 1 can chickpeas, drained & rinsed
- 1 tbsp olive oil
- 2 tbsp balsamic vinegar
- 1 tsp honey (or maple syrup)
- 1/2 tsp smoked paprika
- 1/2 tsp garlic powder
- 1/4 tsp salt

Directions:

(1) Heat the steam oven to 375°F, or 190°C, with the convection and steam functions turned on. (2) Once the chickpeas are dry, pat them down and mix them with salt, garlic powder, olive oil, balsamic vinegar, honey, and paprika. (3) Distribute evenly onto a baking sheet. (4) To get evenly crisped edges, shake the pan halfway during roasting. (5) Allow it to cool for a moment before you eat. Try it as a garnish for your salad or a snack.

119. Thai Coconut Chicken Soup

Total Time: 35 minutes | Prep Time: 10 minutes

Ingredients:

- 1 lb boneless chicken breast, thinly sliced
- 3 cups chicken broth
- 1 can (13.5 oz) coconut milk
- 2 stalks lemongrass, chopped
- Three kaffir lime leaves (or zest of 1 lime)
- 1-inch ginger, sliced
- 1 tbsp fish sauce
- 1 tbsp lime juice
- 1 tsp red curry paste
- 1 cup mushrooms, sliced
- 1 red chili, sliced (optional)
- 1/4 cup fresh cilantro for garnish

Directions:

(1) Start the steam oven at 212 degrees Fahrenheit (100 degrees Celsius). (2) Gather all the ingredients in a bowl that can withstand steaming, including chicken broth, coconut milk, ginger, lime leaves, curry paste, fish sauce, and lemongrass. (3) Infuse flavors by steaming for 15 minutes. (4) Saute the mushrooms and sliced chicken for 10 more minutes or until the chicken is cooked through. (5) Garnish with cilantro and chile, and serve after removing the ginger slices and lime leaves.

120. Pesto Stuffed Bell Peppers

Total Time: 35 minutes | Prep Time: 10 minutes

Ingredients:

- 4 bell peppers, halved and seeds removed
- 1 cup cooked quinoa
- 1/2 cup cherry tomatoes, diced
- 1/4 cup basil pesto
- 1/2 cup mozzarella cheese, shredded
- 1/4 cup parmesan cheese, grated
- 1/4 tsp salt
- 1/4 tsp black pepper

Directions:

(1) On steam mode, bring the steam oven up to 212°F, or 100°C. (2) Combine the quinoa, cherry tomatoes, pesto, salt, and pepper in a single bowl. (3) Distribute the filling evenly among the bell pepper halves. (4) After stuffing the peppers, steam them for 20 minutes in a dish that can withstand steam. (5) Add the Parmesan and mozzarella cheeses, then melt them in the oven for 5 minutes using a combined steam and convection setting set to 400°F (200°C). (6) Keep heated before serving.

121. Creamy Avocado and Lemon Pasta

Total Time: 25 minutes | Prep Time: 10 minutes | Cook Time: 15 minutes

Ingredients:

12 oz spaghetti or fettuccine	1 ripe avocado, pitted and peeled
2 tbsp lemon juice	1/2 cup Greek yogurt
2 cloves garlic, minced	1/4 cup grated Parmesan cheese
1/4 cup fresh basil, chopped	1/2 tsp salt
1/4 tsp black pepper	1/4 tsp red pepper flakes (optional)
1/4 cup cherry tomatoes, halved	1/4 cup pine nuts (optional)

Directions:

(1) Turn your steam oven on to 212 degrees Fahrenheit (100 degrees Celsius). (2) If using a steam oven, cook the pasta for 12–15 minutes on a perforated pan until it reaches the desired doneness. Reserve the drained liquid. (3) Combine the avocado, lemon juice, Greek yogurt, garlic, Parmesan, salt, and black pepper to make the sauce. Blend until well combined. (4) Mix the spaghetti with the sauce, adding a little of the pasta water that was set aside as necessary. (5) Sprinkle with red pepper flakes, pine nuts, cherry tomatoes, and fresh basil for garnish. Serve right away.

122. Greek Stuffed Peppers

Total Time: 40 minutes | Prep Time: 15 minutes | Cook Time: 25 minutes

Ingredients:

4 large bell peppers (any color), halved & seeded	1 cup cooked quinoa
1/2 cup crumbled feta cheese	1/2 cup cherry tomatoes, diced
1/4 cup Kalamata olives, sliced	1/4 cup red onion, diced
1 tsp dried oregano	2 tbsp olive oil
1/2 tsp salt	1/4 tsp black pepper

Directions:

(1) On steam mode, bring the steam oven up to 212°F, or 100°C. (2) Quinoa, feta, cherry tomatoes, olives, red onion, oregano, olive oil, salt, and black pepper make up the filling. Combine all of the ingredients in a bowl. (3) After stuffing the peppers, put them in a baking dish that can withstand steam. (4) After 25 minutes of steaming, the peppers should be soft. (5) Warm the dish and top with more feta and fresh herbs, if preferred.

123. Balsamic Glazed Carrots

Total Time: 30 minutes | Prep Time: 10 minutes | Cook Time: 20 minutes

Ingredients:

1 lb baby carrots	2 tbsp balsamic vinegar
1 tbsp honey or maple syrup	1 tbsp olive oil

1/2 tsp salt   1/4 tsp black pepper

1/2 tsp dried thyme

Directions:

(1) On steam mode, bring the steam oven up to 212°F, or 100°C. (2) Put the carrots in a baking dish that can withstand steam. (3) Permit to steam for fifteen minutes or until soft. (4) Make the glaze by whisking together the balsamic vinegar, honey, olive oil, salt, pepper, & thyme in a bowl. (5) Before steaming for a further 5 minutes, toss the carrots with the glaze. (6) Warm it up and top it with some fresh thyme if you want.

124. Thai Basil Chicken and Vegetables

Total Time: 35 minutes | Prep Time: 15 minutes | Cook Time: 20 minutes

Ingredients:

2 boneless, skinless chicken breasts, thinly sliced	1 cup snap peas
1 red bell pepper, sliced	1 carrot, julienned
2 tbsp soy sauce	1 tbsp fish sauce
1 tbsp honey	1 tsp chili flakes (optional)
1/2 tsp garlic powder	1/4 cup fresh Thai basil leaves

Directions:

(1) On steam mode, bring the steam oven up to 212°F, or 100°C. (2) Sauce ingredients include soy sauce, fish sauce, honey, garlic powder, and chili flakes. (3) Put the veggies and chicken in a pan that can withstand steam. (4) Cook for 15 minutes in the steamer before adding the sauce and continuing to steam for five more minutes. (5) Before serving hot over steamed rice, top with fresh Thai basil.

125. Baked Sweet Potato and Kale Salad

Total Time: 40 minutes | Prep Time: 10 minutes | Cook Time: 30 minutes

Ingredients:

2 medium sweet potatoes, peeled and diced	2 cups kale, chopped
1/4 cup pecans, toasted	1/4 cup dried cranberries
1/4 cup feta cheese, crumbled	2 tbsp olive oil
1 tbsp maple syrup	1 tsp Dijon mustard
1 tbsp apple cider vinegar	1/2 tsp salt
1/4 tsp black pepper	

Directions:

(1) Switch to the steam-bake setting and heat the oven to 180 degrees Celsius. (2) After brushing the sweet potatoes with the olive oil, toss them to coat them in a baking dish. Cook in a steam oven for 25 minutes. The remaining olive oil, salt, pepper, Dijon mustard, maple syrup, and apple cider vinegar are whisked together to make the dressing. (3) After 3 minutes of steaming, the kale should be somewhat wilted. (4) Combine the kale, sweet potatoes, cranberries, pecans, and feta in a salad bowl. Toss with the dressing and serve while still warm.

126. Sweet Potato and Chickpea Stew

Total Time: 45 minutes | Prep Time: 15 minutes

Ingredients:

- 2 medium sweet potatoes, peeled and diced
- 1 can (14 oz) diced tomatoes
- 2 cloves garlic, minced
- 1 tsp ground cumin
- ½ tsp smoked paprika
- Salt and black pepper to taste
- 1 tbsp olive oil
- 1 can chickpeas, drained & rinsed
- 1 small onion, diced
- 2 cups vegetable broth
- 1 tsp ground coriander
- ½ tsp ground cinnamon
- 1 cup baby spinach

Directions:

(1) The steam oven has to be preheated to 212°F, or 100°C, with full steam. (2) Spice up your sweet potato and chickpea meal by adding chopped tomatoes, onion, garlic, and vegetable broth. Don't forget to add the heatproof dish. Be sure to mix well. (3) To get soft sweet potatoes, prepare the meal in a steam oven for 30 minutes. (4) After the first 5 minutes of steaming, add the baby spinach & continue cooking un till the spinach wilts. (5) Olive oil, salt, and pepper are the finishing touches. Hot is best.

127. Balsamic Roasted Vegetables

Total Time: 30 minutes | Prep Time: 10 minutes

Ingredients:

- 1 zucchini, sliced
- 1 yellow bell pepper, sliced
- 1 red onion, sliced
- 1 red bell pepper, sliced
- 1 small eggplant, diced
- 2 tbsp balsamic vinegar
- 1 tbsp olive oil
- ½ tsp garlic powder
- 1 tsp dried oregano
- Salt and black pepper to taste

Directions:

(1) Set the steam oven to a temperature of 400°F, or 200°C, using a mixture of steam and convection steam. (2) Combine the veggies in a big basin and add the balsamic vinegar, olive oil, oregano, garlic powder, salt, and black pepper. Season to taste. (3) On a baking sheet, arrange the veggies in one layer. (4) The veggies should be cooked until they are soft and slightly caramelized, which should take around 20 minutes in a steam oven, stirring once halfway through. (5) Warm it up and serve it with quinoa or as a side.

128. Thai Green Curry Chicken

Total Time: 40 minutes | Prep Time: 15 minutes

Ingredients:

- 2 boneless, skinless chicken breasts, sliced
- 2 tbsp Thai green curry paste
- 1 red bell pepper, sliced
- 2 tsp fish sauce
- 1 tbsp lime juice
- 1 can (14 oz) coconut milk
- 1 small zucchini, sliced
- 1 cup snow peas
- 1 tsp brown sugar
- Fresh basil or cilantro for garnish

Directions:

(1) A steam oven preheated to 100% steam should reach 212°F or 100°C. (2) The ingredients for the green curry paste, fish sauce, lime juice, brown sugar, & coconut milk should be mixed in a heatproof dish. (3) After adding the red bell pepper, zucchini, and sliced

chicken to the dish, mix and combine. (4) To ensure the chicken is cooked through, steam it for 25 minutes. (5) Toss in the snow peas and continue steaming for another five minutes. (6) Serve over jasmine rice that has been cooked and top with fresh cilantro or basil.

129. Creamy Spinach and Lemon Pasta

Total Time: 30 minutes | Prep Time: 10 minutes

Ingredients:

- 8 oz pasta (penne or fettuccine)
- 2 cups baby spinach
- 1 cup heavy cream or coconut cream
- ½ cup grated Parmesan cheese
- 2 cloves garlic, minced
- 1 tbsp lemon zest
- 1 tbsp lemon juice
- 1 tbsp olive oil
- Salt and black pepper to taste

Directions:

(1) A steam oven preheated to 100% steam should reach 212°F or 100°C. (2) Add enough water to cover the pasta in a steam-safe dish. Place in a steamer and cook for 15 minutes or until carrots are tender but still firm. Run off. (3) To make the lemon zest and juice, as well as the heavy cream, garlic, and Parmesan cheese, set aside in their own dish. (4) After five minutes of steaming, combine the baby spinach and cooked pasta. (5) After the first 5 minutes of steaming, add five more minutes to let the spinach wilt and the sauce thicken. (6) Warm it up, drizzle it with olive oil, and add some salt and pepper.

130. Mediterranean Quinoa and Chickpea Salad

Total Time: 25 minutes | Prep Time: 10 minutes

Ingredients:

- 1 cup quinoa, rinsed
- 1 can chickpeas, drained & rinsed
- 1 small cucumber, diced
- ½ cup cherry tomatoes, halved
- ¼ cup red onion, finely chopped
- ¼ cup crumbled feta cheese (optional)
- ¼ cup fresh parsley, chopped
- 2 tbsp olive oil
- 1 tbsp lemon juice
- 1 tsp dried oregano
- Salt and black pepper to taste

Directions:

(1) A steam oven preheated to 100% steam should reach 212°F or 100°C. (2) Put two cups of water & 2 cups of steam-safe quinoa in a bowl. To make the fluffier, steam for 20 minutes. Allow to cool down a little. (3) Throw the cooked quinoa, chickpeas, cucumber, cherry tomatoes, red onion, and parsley into a big bowl and stir to blend. (4) After that, add some lemon juice and olive oil, & then season with salt, pepper, & oregano. Toss gently. (5) When serving, garnish with crumbled feta cheese and let cool or serve cold.

131. Spinach and Feta Stuffed Zucchini

Total Time: 40 minutes | Prep Time: 10 minutes

Ingredients:

- 4 medium zucchinis
- 2 cups fresh spinach, chopped

1 cup feta cheese, crumbled	1/4 cup breadcrumbs
1/4 cup grated Parmesan cheese	1 tablespoon olive oil
2 cloves garlic, minced	Salt and pepper, to taste

Directions:

(1) A steam oven should be preheated to 375°F, or 190°C. (2) To make boats, cut zucchinis lengthwise and remove seeds. (3) Sauté the garlic in olive oil for around a minute over medium heat or until it begins to release its aromatic aroma. (4) After two or three minutes, add the spinach and simmer until it wilts. Get it out of the oven. (5) The cooked spinach, feta, breadcrumbs, Parmesan, salt, & pepper should all be combined in a bowl. (6) Fill the zucchini boats with the mixture using a spoon. (7) Cook the filled zucchinis for 20 to 25 minutes in a steam oven until they are soft. (8) Keep heated before serving.

132. Thai Curry Cauliflower

Total Time: 30 minutes | Prep Time: 10 minutes

Ingredients:

1 medium cauliflower, cut into florets	2 tablespoons red curry paste
1 can (14 oz) coconut milk	1 tablespoon soy sauce
1 teaspoon lime juice	1 tablespoon olive oil
Fresh cilantro, chopped (for garnish)	Salt to taste

Directions:

(1) A steam oven should be preheated to 375°F, or 190°C. (2) Combine the florets of cauliflower, olive oil, and salt in a bowl. (3) Prepare the curry paste by whisking together the coconut milk, lime juice, soy sauce, and curry paste in a small bowl. (4) Once steamed, place the cauliflower in an oven-safe dish and drizzle with curry sauce. (5) Cauliflower should be steamed for 20 minutes or until done. (6) Before serving, top with chopped fresh cilantro.

133. Balsamic Roasted Chicken Thighs

Total Time: 45 minutes | Prep Time: 10 minutes

Ingredients:

4 bone-in chicken thighs	1/4 cup balsamic vinegar
2 tablespoons olive oil	1 teaspoon honey
2 cloves garlic, minced	1 teaspoon dried rosemary
Salt and pepper, to taste	

Directions:

(1) A steam oven should be preheated to 400°F or 200°C. (2) Combine olive oil, balsamic vinegar, honey, garlic, rosemary, salt, and pepper in a mixing bowl. (3) Marinate the chicken thighs for at least ten to fifteen minutes. (4) After 30–35 minutes of roasting in the steam oven, the chicken thighs are done. (5) Top with your preferred side and serve hot.

134. Balsamic Glazed Brussels Sprouts

Total Time: 30 minutes | Prep Time: 10 minutes

Ingredients:

- 2 cups Brussels sprouts, halved
- 2 tablespoons balsamic vinegar
- 1 tablespoon olive oil
- 1 teaspoon honey
- Salt and pepper, to taste

Directions:

(1) A steam oven should be preheated to 375°F, or 190°C. (2) Before tossing the Brussels sprouts with the dressing, combine the olive oil, balsamic vinegar, honey, salt, & pepper. Add the Brussels sprouts to a plate that can be used in a steam oven. (3) To get a soft and caramelized texture, steam for 20-25 minutes. (4) Keep heated before serving.

135. Roasted Sweet Potatoes with Maple Syrup

Total Time: 40 minutes | Prep Time: 10 minutes

Ingredients:

- Four medium sweet potatoes peeled & cut into cubes
- 2 tablespoons olive oil
- 2 tablespoons maple syrup
- 1/2 teaspoon cinnamon
- Salt and pepper, to taste

Directions:

(1) Bring the temperature of the steam oven up to 375°F, which is 190°C. (2) Dress the cubes of sweet potato with a mixture of olive oil, maple syrup, cinnamon, salt, and pepper. (3) Using parchment paper, arrange the sweet potatoes on a baking sheet. (4) Cook in a steam oven for 30–35 minutes or until soft and browned. (5) Warm it up and give it out as an appetizer or first course.

136. Lemon Dill Cod

Total Time: 20 minutes | Prep Time: 5 minutes

Ingredients:

- 2 cod fillets (6 oz each)
- 1 tablespoon olive oil
- 1 tablespoon lemon juice
- 1 teaspoon lemon zest
- 1 teaspoon fresh dill, chopped
- ½ teaspoon garlic powder
- Salt and pepper to taste
- 2 lemon slices

Directions:

(1) Bring the steam oven up to 85% steam and 350°F (175°C) before using it. (2) Apply paper towels to blot the cod fillets. (3) Combine olive oil, parsley, garlic powder, lemon zest, lemon juice, & pepper in a small bowl. (4) Place the fish fillets in a steam-proof baking dish & sprinkle with a mixture of dill & lemon. Place a slice of lemon on top of each fillet. (5) To get opaque flesh and easy flaking, steam the fish for 12–15 minutes. (6) Quickly accompanied with rice and steamed veggies.

137. Spaghetti Squash with Marinara Sauce

Total Time: 40 minutes | Prep Time: 10 minutes

Ingredients:

- 1 medium spaghetti squash, halved & seeds removed
- 1 tablespoon olive oil
- ½ teaspoon salt
- ¼ teaspoon black pepper
- 2 cups marinara sauce
- ½ teaspoon Italian seasoning

| ¼ cup grated Parmesan cheese (optional) | Fresh basil for garnish |

Directions:

(1) Get the steam oven up to temperature, then set it to 400°F or 200°C. (2) Season the squash cutlets with salt and pepper & coat them with olive oil. In a baking dish that can withstand steam, lay the squash halves cut side down. (3) After 30 minutes of steaming, the flesh should be soft enough to shred with a fork. (4) At the same time, add the Italian spice to the marinara sauce and heat it up. (5) Toss the squash strands with the marinara sauce after scraping them with a fork. (6) Accompany with freshly chopped basil and Parmesan cheese.

138. Garlic Butter Shrimp Scampi

Total Time: 15 minutes | Prep Time: 5 minutes

Ingredients:

1 pound large shrimp, peeled and deveined	2 tablespoons unsalted butter, melted
1 tablespoon olive oil	3 cloves garlic, minced
½ teaspoon red pepper flakes (optional)	½ teaspoon salt
¼ teaspoon black pepper	2 tablespoons fresh parsley, chopped
Juice of 1 lemon	8 oz cooked linguine (optional)

Directions:

(1) Steam the oven to 85% capacity at 350°F, or 175°C. (2) Combine the shrimp with melted butter, olive oil, garlic, red pepper flakes, salt, & black pepper in a dish that can withstand steaming. (3) Skewer the shrimp until they're pink and opaque, then steam for 7 to 10 minutes. (4) Before serving, squeeze some lemon juice & garnish with chopped fresh parsley. (5) Placé over top of cooked linguine or with toasted bread.

139. Spinach and Ricotta Stuffed Shells

Total Time: 40 minutes | Prep Time: 15 minutes

Ingredients:

12 jumbo pasta shells, cooked al dente	1 cup ricotta cheese
½ cup shredded mozzarella cheese	¼ cup grated Parmesan cheese
1 cup fresh spinach, chopped	1 egg, lightly beaten
1 teaspoon garlic powder	½ teaspoon salt
¼ teaspoon black pepper	1½ cups marinara sauce

Directions:

(1) Set the steam oven to 375°F, or 190°C, for full steam. (2) Combine ricotta, mozzarella, Parmesan, spinach, egg, garlic powder, salt, and black pepper in a bowl. (3) Spoon the ricotta mixture into each pasta shell. (4) Transfer half of the marinara sauce to a baking dish that can withstand steam. Top with the filled shells and drizzle with the remaining sauce. (5) Melt and bubble the cheese by steaming for 20 minutes. (6) Top with more Parmesan and chopped basil before serving.

140. Garlic Herb Roasted Turkey Breast

Total Time: 1 hour 15 minutes | Prep Time: 10 minutes

Ingredients:

1 (3-pound) boneless turkey breast, skin-on	2 tablespoons olive oil
2 tablespoons unsalted butter, melted	3 cloves garlic, minced
1 teaspoon dried thyme	1 teaspoon dried rosemary
1 teaspoon salt	½ teaspoon black pepper
½ cup chicken broth	

Directions:

(1) Bring the steam oven up to 375°F, or 190°C, with 50% steam. (2) Combine the garlic, thyme, rosemary, olive oil, butter, salt, and black pepper in a small bowl. (3) After drying the turkey breast, massage it all over with the herb mixture. (4) Put the turkey and chicken broth in a roasting pan that can withstand steam. (5) The internal heat should reach 74°C after 60-75 minutes of roasting, with basting done halfway through. (6) After 10 minutes, let aside to cool before cutting.

141. Lemon Basil Pasta

Total Time: 25 minutes | Prep Time: 10 minutes

Ingredients:

12 oz pasta (penne or spaghetti)	2 cups cherry tomatoes, halved
2 tbsp olive oil	2 garlic cloves, minced
Zest and juice of 1 lemon	½ cup fresh basil leaves, chopped
½ cup grated Parmesan cheese	Salt and black pepper to taste

Directions:

(1) Bring the steam oven up to temperature, then turn it on full steam. (2) Cover the pasta with water and set it in a steam-safe dish. Cook in a steamer for 8 to 10 minutes or until the pasta is soft and bite-able. Reserve the drained liquid. (3) Put the cherry tomatoes in a separate steam-safe dish and add the garlic, olive oil, salt, and pepper. Cook until tender, about 5 minutes, in a steamer. (4) Pasta, roasted tomatoes, zest, juice, and fresh basil should all be combined in a big basin. Toss gently. (5) Top with grated Parmesan and serve while still warm.

142. Spaghetti with Roasted Tomato Sauce

Total Time: 40 minutes | Prep Time: 10 minutes

Ingredients:

12 oz spaghetti	4 large tomatoes, quartered
3 garlic cloves, minced	1 tbsp olive oil
1 tsp dried oregano	½ tsp red pepper flakes (optional)
Salt and black pepper to taste	½ cup fresh basil, chopped

Directions:

(1) Turn the steam oven's combined steam setting to 350°F (180°C) to begin preheating. (2) Put the tomatoes in a baking dish that can withstand steam, then add the olive oil, garlic, oregano, salt, and pepper. Cook until tender, about 25 minutes. (3) Pasta should be cooked for eight to ten minutes in a steam oven set to 212 degrees Fahrenheit (100 degrees Celsius). Reserve the drained liquid. (4) To make a smooth sauce, blend the roasted tomatoes. If you like a chunkier texture, smash them with a fork. (5) Toss the spaghetti with the sauce after it's cooked, then sprinkle fresh basil on top.

143. Spinach and Mushroom Stuffed Mushrooms

Total Time: 30 minutes | Prep Time: 15 minutes

Ingredients:

- 12 large button mushrooms, stems removed
- ½ cup mushrooms stems, finely chopped
- ¼ cup grated Parmesan cheese
- 1 tbsp olive oil
- 1 cup fresh spinach, chopped
- ½ cup cream cheese, softened
- 1 garlic clove, minced
- Salt and black pepper to taste

Directions:

(1) Turn the steam oven's combined steam setting to 350°F (180°C) to begin preheating. (2) In a skillet over middle heat, sauté the chopped stems of mushrooms and garlic for two minutes with the olive oil. (3) Toss in the spinach and sauté until it wilts. Whisk in the cream cheese, Parmesan, pepper, and salt after taking it from the stove. (4) After stuffing the mushroom caps with the spinach mixture, place them on a platter that can withstand steam. After 12 to 15 minutes of steaming, the mushrooms should be soft. Keep heated before serving.

144. Roasted Veggie and Quinoa Salad

Total Time: 35 minutes | Prep Time: 15 minutes

Ingredients:

- 1 cup quinoa
- 2 cups water
- 1 zucchini, diced
- 1 cup cherry tomatoes, halved
- 1 tsp dried oregano
- ½ cup crumbled feta cheese (optional)
- 1 red bell pepper, diced
- 1 tbsp olive oil
- Salt and black pepper to taste
- 2 tbsp balsamic vinegar

Directions:

(1) Turn the steam oven on high heat and get it up to 212 degrees Fahrenheit (100 degrees Celsius). (2) After giving the quinoa a quick rinse in cold water, soak it for 15 minutes in a steam-safe pot with 2 cups of water. After fluffing with a fork, put aside. (3) Combine the cherry tomatoes, bell pepper, zucchini, & olive oil in a separate dish & season with salt & pepper. Add the oregano. Sauté in a combined steam oven at 350°F (180°C) for around 15 to 20 minutes. (4) Toss the quinoa with the roasted vegetables and top with the balsamic vinegar. (5) Feel free to garnish with feta cheese before serving, either heated or cooled.

145. Balsamic Roasted Cauliflower

Total Time: 30 minutes | Prep Time: 10 minutes

Ingredients:

- 1 head cauliflower, cut into florets
- 1 tbsp balsamic vinegar
- ½ tsp smoked paprika
- ¼ cup chopped fresh parsley (for garnish)
- 2 tbsp olive oil
- 1 tsp garlic powder
- Salt and black pepper to taste

Directions:

(1) Set the steam oven to combined steam and heat it to 375°F, or 190°C. (2) Throw the cauliflower florets into a large bowl and toss with garlic powder, smoked paprika, olive oil, balsamic vinegar, salt, & pepper. Roast, tossing halfway through, the cauliflower for 20 to 25 minutes, or until soft & browned, on a steam-safe baking sheet. (3) Serve heated with a sprinkle of fresh parsley for garnish.

146. Chicken Parmesan

Total Time: 35 minutes | Prep Time: 10 minutes

Ingredients:

- 2 boneless, skinless chicken breasts
- ½ teaspoon salt
- ½ teaspoon black pepper
- ½ teaspoon garlic powder
- ½ teaspoon onion powder
- ½ cup marinara sauce
- ½ cup shredded mozzarella cheese
- ¼ cup grated Parmesan cheese
- ½ cup panko breadcrumbs
- 1 teaspoon dried oregano
- 1 teaspoon olive oil
- Fresh basil for garnish

Directions:

(1) Turn the steam oven's combined steam setting to 350°F (180°C) to begin preheating. (2) Onion powder, salt, pepper, garlic powder, & chicken breasts need to be mixed together. Combine the olive oil, oregano, Parmesan cheese, and panko breadcrumbs in a small bowl. (3) Arrange the chicken pieces on a steam oven dish with holes in it and drizzle with marinara sauce. Mix the breadcrumbs and sprinkle them on top. (4) Bring the interior temperature to 165°F (75°C) by steam-baking for 25 minutes. (5) After five more minutes in the oven, top the chicken with the mozzarella cheese and continue cooking until the cheese melts and bubbles. (6) Before serving while still hot, top with fresh basil.

147. Curried Cauliflower

Total Time: 30 minutes | Prep Time: 10 minutes

Ingredients:

- 1 head cauliflower, cut into florets
- 2 tablespoons olive oil
- 1 teaspoon ground turmeric
- 1 teaspoon ground cumin
- 1 teaspoon ground coriander
- ½ teaspoon salt
- ½ teaspoon black pepper
- ½ teaspoon chili powder (optional)
- ¼ cup coconut milk
- Fresh cilantro for garnish

Directions:

(1) Start the steam oven's convection heating system at 375°F, or 190°C. (2) Combine the cauliflower florets with the balsamic vinegar, olive oil, turmeric, cumin, coriander, salt, & pepper in a mixing bowl. Evenly distribute the spiced cauliflower across a steam oven baking sheet, and roast for twenty minutes. (3) Toss the cauliflower with the coconut milk and continue roasting for an additional 5 minutes. (4) Serve while still heated, topped with chopped fresh cilantro.

148. Creamy Tomato Basil Pasta

Total Time: 25 minutes | Prep Time: 5 minutes

Ingredients:

- 8 oz pasta (penne or fusilli)
- 1 ½ cups cherry tomatoes, halved
- 1 teaspoon olive oil
- ½ teaspoon salt

½ teaspoon black pepper

½ teaspoon garlic powder

1 cup heavy cream

½ cup grated Parmesan cheese

½ cup fresh basil leaves, chopped

Directions:

(1) The steam oven should be preheated to full steam at 200°F or 90°C. (2) Toss the pasta with enough water to cover in a steam-safe dish. After 12–15 minutes of steaming, when the pasta is still somewhat firm, drain. (3) Coat the cherry tomatoes with olive oil, season with salt & pepper, & add garlic powder. With a separate oven-safe dish, cook for 10 minutes at 180°C or until they are soft. Combine with Parmesan cheese and heavy cream. To thicken the sauce, put it back in the oven for 5 minutes. (4) Incorporate the cooked spaghetti into the rich tomato sauce. Serve heated with a sprinkle of fresh basil.

149. Thai Basil Chicken

Total Time: 25 minutes | Prep Time: 10 minutes

Ingredients:

Two tiny slices of skinless, boneless chicken breasts

2 tablespoons soy sauce

1 tablespoon oyster sauce

1 teaspoon fish sauce

1 teaspoon brown sugar

½ teaspoon chili flakes (optional)

1 tablespoon olive oil

2 cloves garlic, minced

½ cup fresh Thai basil leaves

Directions:

(1) Turn the steam oven's combined steam setting to 350°F (180°C) to begin preheating. (2) Combine five sauces—soy, oyster, fish, brown sugar, and chili flakes—in a small dish. (3) Combine olive oil, minced garlic, and chicken in a steam-safe dish. Toss to coat. Coat the chicken with the sauce mixture. (4) Steam-bake for fifteen minutes, tossing once while cooking. (5) Cook, stirring occasionally, for two more minutes or until the fresh Thai basil leaves wilt. (6) Top with steaming rice and serve.

150. Sweet and Spicy Roasted Nuts

Total Time: 20 minutes | Prep Time: 5 minutes

Ingredients:

2 cups mixed nuts (almonds, cashews, pecans)

2 tablespoons maple syrup

1 teaspoon olive oil

½ teaspoon ground cinnamon

½ teaspoon chili powder

¼ teaspoon cayenne pepper

½ teaspoon salt

Directions:

(1) Set the steam oven to convection steam mode and heat it to 325°F or 160°C. (2) Combine olive oil, salt, cinnamon, chili powder, and maple syrup in a bowl. (3) Coat the nuts evenly by tossing them in the mixture. (4) Ensure that the nuts are evenly distributed over a steam oven pan. Cook, turning once, for fifteen minutes. (5) Allow to cool entirely before consumption.

151. Greek Quinoa Salad

Total Time: 25 minutes | Prep Time: 10 minutes

Ingredients:

Ingredients:

- 1 cup quinoa, rinsed
- 2 cups water
- 1/2 cup cherry tomatoes, halved
- 1/2 cup cucumber, diced
- 1/4 cup red onion, finely chopped
- 1/4 cup Kalamata olives, sliced
- 1/4 cup feta cheese, crumbled
- 2 tbsp olive oil
- 1 tbsp red wine vinegar
- 1 tsp dried oregano
- Salt and pepper to taste

Directions:

(1) Set the steam oven to 212°F, which is 100°C. (2) Fill a pot that can withstand steam with water and quinoa. After 15 minutes of steaming, the quinoa should be soft and have absorbed most of the water. Give it some time to cool. (3) After the quinoa has cooled, throw in some cucumber, tomatoes, red onion, olives, and feta cheese in a big bowl. (4) Combine the oregano, salt, pepper, red wine vinegar, olive oil, and a small bowl and whisk to combine. (5) Mix the quinoa with the dressing and toss to combine. (6) Put in the fridge to make a cold salad or serve right away.

152. Roasted Beet Salad

Total Time: 40 minutes | Prep Time: 10 minutes

Ingredients:

- 3 medium beets, peeled and diced
- 2 tbsp olive oil
- 1/2 tsp salt
- 1/4 tsp black pepper
- 1/4 cup goat cheese, crumbled
- 1/4 cup walnuts, toasted
- 2 cups mixed greens
- 2 tbsp balsamic vinegar

Directions:

(1) A steam oven should be preheated to 375°F, or 190°C. (2) Whisk together the olive oil, salt, & pepper with the diced beets. Arrange in a roasting pan that can withstand steam. (3) Cook in a steam oven until soft when prodded with a fork, about 30 minutes. Allow to cool down a little. (4) Spread a bed of mixed greens out on a platter. Crumbled goat cheese, walnuts, and roasted beets make a tasty topping. (5) Just before serving, drizzle with balsamic vinegar.

153. Greek Stuffed Portobello Mushrooms

Total Time: 30 minutes | Prep Time: 10 minutes

Ingredients:

- 4 large Portobello mushrooms, stems removed
- 1 cup fresh spinach, chopped
- 1/2 cup cherry tomatoes, diced
- 1/4 cup Kalamata olives, chopped
- 1/4 cup feta cheese, crumbled
- 1 tbsp olive oil
- 1 clove garlic, minced
- 1/2 tsp dried oregano
- Salt and pepper to taste

Directions:

(1) A steam oven should be preheated to 375°F, or 190°C. (2) Apply olive oil to the Portobello mushrooms and set them on a steam-safe plate. (3) Put the spinach, tomatoes, olives, feta cheese, garlic, oregano, salt, and pepper into a bowl. Keep stirring until well combined. (4) Place a small amount of the mixture on the top of each mushroom. After 20 minutes of roasting in the steam oven, the mushrooms should be soft. (5) Warm it up and enjoy it as an entree or appetizer.

154. Roasted Garlic Brussels Sprouts

Total Time: 35 minutes | Prep Time: 10 minutes

Ingredients:

1 lb Brussels sprouts, trimmed and halved	2 tbsp olive oil
3 cloves garlic, minced	1/2 tsp salt
1/4 tsp black pepper	1 tbsp balsamic glaze (optional)

Directions:

(1) A steam oven should be preheated to 400°F or 200°C. (2) Add garlic, salt, pepper, olive oil, and Brussels sprouts; toss to combine. (3) Make sure your roasting pan can withstand steam before spreading it out. (4) To get a golden brown and crispy texture, roast for 25 minutes while stirring once halfway through. (5) Before serving, drizzle with balsamic glaze if preferred.

155. Roasted Stuffed Mushrooms

Total Time: 30 minutes | Prep Time: 10 minutes

Ingredients:

12 large white mushrooms, stems removed	1/2 cup cream cheese, softened
1/4 cup grated Parmesan cheese	1/4 cup breadcrumbs
1 clove garlic, minced	1 tbsp fresh parsley, chopped
1 tbsp olive oil	1/2 tsp salt
1/4 tsp black pepper	

Directions:

(1) A steam oven should be preheated to 375°F, or 190°C. (2) Combine flour, garlic, Parmesan, breadcrumbs, salt, pepper, and cream cheese in a bowl. (3) Distribute the cheese mixture among the mushroom caps one by one. (4) Season with olive oil and set on a baking sheet that can withstand steam. (5) To get the soft and golden roast, roast for 20 minutes. (6) Warm it up and serve it as an appetizer.

156. Creamy Lemon Herb Pasta

Total Time: 30 minutes | Prep Time: 10 minutes

Ingredients:

12 oz pasta (fettuccine or penne)	1 ½ cups heavy cream
1 cup grated Parmesan cheese	2 tbsp unsalted butter
1 tbsp olive oil	2 cloves garlic, minced
Zest and juice of 1 lemon	1 tsp dried oregano
1 tsp dried basil	½ tsp salt
¼ tsp black pepper	1 cup steamed peas (optional)
¼ cup chopped fresh parsley	

Directions:

(1) Turn on the steam setting and heat the oven to 210°F, or 100°C. (2) Toss the pasta with the boiling water in a pan that can withstand steam. Bring to a boil & cook for ten minutes or until the bite is just right. Reserve the drained liquid. (3) Put the garlic, olive oil, & butter in a

pot that can withstand steam. Cook the garlic in a steamer for three minutes or until it releases its aroma. (4) Garnish with oregano, basil, salt, pepper, lemon zest, lemon juice, and heavy cream. Poach for 5 minutes, tossing every so often. (5) Toss in the Parmesan and mix until combined. Add three more minutes of steaming time to thicken. (6) Add steamed peas (if used) and toss the cooked pasta with the sauce. (7) Warm and top with fresh parsley.

157. Thai Green Curry Shrimp

Total Time: 35 minutes | Prep Time: 15 minutes

Ingredients:

- 1 lb large shrimp, peeled and deveined
- 1 can (13.5 oz) coconut milk
- 2 tbsp Thai green curry paste
- 1 tbsp fish sauce
- 1 tbsp soy sauce
- 1 tbsp brown sugar
- 1 cup diced bell peppers (any color)
- 1 cup snap peas
- 1 small zucchini, sliced
- ½ cup chopped fresh basil
- 1 lime, cut into wedges
- 1 cup steamed jasmine rice (for serving)

Directions:

(1) Turn on the steam setting and heat the oven to 200°F, or 93°C. (2) Combine the green curry paste, coconut milk, fish sauce, soy sauce, & brown sugar in a basin that can withstand steam. Whisk to combine. (3) Toss in some zucchini, snap peas, and bell peppers with the sauce. Cook in a steamer for 10 minutes or until just softened. (4) Put the shrimp in and mix it up. To get perfectly cooked and pink shrimp, steam for 8 to 10 minutes. (5) Pour hot over jasmine rice that has been cooked, top with fresh basil, and garnish with lime wedges.

158. Caprese Stuffed Chicken

Total Time: 40 minutes | Prep Time: 15 minutes

Ingredients:

- 4 boneless, skinless chicken breasts
- 1 cup fresh mozzarella, sliced
- 1 cup cherry tomatoes, halved
- ¼ cup fresh basil leaves
- 2 tbsp olive oil
- 1 tsp balsamic glaze
- ½ tsp salt
- ½ tsp black pepper
- 1 tsp Italian seasoning

Directions:

(1) The steam oven has to be heated up to 215°F, or 102°C. (2) In order to make a pocket in each chicken breast, slice them lengthwise, but do not cut through. (3) Layer fresh basil, cherry tomatoes, and mozzarella into each pocket. Hold in place with toothpicks if necessary. (4) Toss the chicken with olive oil and add salt, pepper, and Italian seasoning. Season to taste. (5) To achieve an internal heat of 74°C, place the stuffing-filled chicken on a steam-safe plate and steam for 25 minutes. (6) Before serving, heat and drizzle with balsamic glaze.

159. Sweet Potato and Black Bean Enchiladas

Total Time: 45 minutes | Prep Time: 15 minutes

Ingredients:

2 medium sweet potatoes, peeled and diced	1 can black beans, drained & rinsed
1 cup shredded cheddar cheese	1 tsp cumin
1 tsp chili powder	½ tsp garlic powder
½ tsp salt	8 small corn tortillas
1 cup enchilada sauce	¼ cup chopped fresh cilantro

Directions:

(1) Turn on the steam setting and heat the oven to 210°F, or 100°C. (2) After 15 minutes of steaming, the sweet potatoes should be tender. Add black beans, half of the cheese, cumin, chili powder, garlic powder, & salt to the mashed sweet potatoes in a bowl. Mash to combine. (3) Put the filled tortillas on a steam-safe baking dish after filling them with the filling. (4) Spread the tortillas with the enchilada sauce and sprinkle the rest of the cheese on top. (5) Melt and bubble the cheese by steaming for 20 minutes. (6) Before serving, top with chopped fresh cilantro.

160. Ginger-Sesame Chicken

Total Time: 35 minutes | Prep Time: 10 minutes

Ingredients:

4 boneless, skinless chicken thighs	¼ cup soy sauce
1 tbsp sesame oil	1 tbsp honey
1 tbsp rice vinegar	1 tbsp grated fresh ginger
2 cloves garlic, minced	1 tsp sesame seeds
2 green onions, sliced	

Directions:

(1) Set the temperature of the steam oven to 200°F, which is 93°C. (2) In a bowl that can be heated, combine the soy sauce, sesame oil, honey, rice vinegar, garlic, and ginger. Whisk until well combined. (3) Toss the chicken thighs in the coating mixture. Set aside to soak for ten minutes. (4) After the chicken has reached an internal heat of 74°C, move it to a steam-safe dish and steam it for 20 minutes. (5) Sesame seeds and green onions make a lovely garnish.

161. Roasted Stuffed Acorn Squash

Total Time: 45 minutes | Prep Time: 15 minutes

Ingredients:

2 acorn squashes, halved, and seeds removed	1 tablespoon olive oil
½ cup quinoa, rinsed	1 cup vegetable broth
½ teaspoon salt	¼ teaspoon black pepper
½ teaspoon ground cinnamon	¼ teaspoon nutmeg
½ cup dried cranberries	½ cup pecans, chopped
¼ cup feta cheese (optional)	2 tablespoons maple syrup

Directions:

(1) Turn the steam oven onto a combined steam setting (50/50 steam and convection) and heat it to 375°F (190°C). (2) After slicing an acorn squash in half, brush both sides with olive oil and set cut-side up in a baking dish. (3) Cook until just slightly tender, about 20 minutes. (4) As a side note, steam-cook the quinoa for 15 minutes in vegetable stock or until it reaches a soft consistency. (5) After

removing and fluffing with a fork, combine with crushed pecans, salt, pepper, cinnamon, and nutmeg. (6) After 10 further minutes in the steam oven, stuff the quinoa mixture into each squash half. (7) If you're using feta cheese, crumble some on top and drizzle some maple syrup. Keep heated before serving.

162. Butternut Squash Risotto

Total Time: 40 minutes | Prep Time: 10 minutes

Ingredients:

1 cup Arborio rice	2 cups vegetable broth
1 small butternut squash, peeled and diced	½ cup white wine
½ small onion, finely chopped	2 tablespoons olive oil
2 cloves garlic, minced	½ teaspoon salt
¼ teaspoon black pepper	½ teaspoon dried thyme
½ cup Parmesan cheese, grated	2 tablespoons butter

Directions:

(1) Adjust the steam oven's temperature dial to 212 degrees Fahrenheit (100 degrees Celsius). (2) Toss together the Arborio rice, vegetable broth, butternut squash dice, white wine, garlic, olive oil, onion, salt, pepper, and thyme in a skillet that can be used to cook under steam. (3) Put the steam oven cover on and cook for 30 minutes, stirring halfway through. (4) After taking the steam oven out, combine the Parmesan cheese and butter and mix until smooth. (5) If preferred, serve warm with an additional sprinkle of Parmesan.

163. Herb-Crusted Beef Tenderloin

Total Time: 50 minutes | Prep Time: 10 minutes

Ingredients:

1 (2-pound) beef tenderloin, trimmed	2 tablespoons olive oil
1 teaspoon salt	½ teaspoon black pepper
1 tablespoon Dijon mustard	2 cloves garlic, minced
1 tablespoon fresh rosemary, chopped	1 tablespoon fresh thyme, chopped

Directions:

(1) Bring the steam oven up to temperature on the combined steam setting, which is 30% steam and 70% convection, to 275°F, or 135°C. (2) Sprinkle some salt and black pepper on the beef tenderloin and rub it in with olive oil. (3) Garlic, thyme, rosemary, and Dijon mustard should be combined in a small bowl before being applied to the steak. (4) Set the steam oven to medium-rare and cook the tenderloin for 40 minutes, or until it reaches an internal heat of 54°C. (5) Allow 10 minutes to rest after removing from the steam oven, and then slice. Warm it up before plating.

164. Mediterranean Baked Chicken

Total Time: 45 minutes | Prep Time: 15 minutes

Ingredients:

4 boneless, skinless chicken breasts	2 tablespoons olive oil
1 teaspoon salt	½ teaspoon black pepper

1 teaspoon dried oregano	½ teaspoon paprika
1 teaspoon garlic powder	1 cup cherry tomatoes, halved
½ cup Kalamata olives, pitted and sliced	¼ cup feta cheese, crumbled
1 tablespoon lemon juice	

Directions:

(1) Turn the steam oven onto a combined steam setting (50/50 steam and convection) and heat it to 375°F (190°C). (2) Spice up some chicken breasts with a rub of garlic powder, oregano, salt, black pepper, and olive oil. (3) Coat the chicken with olives & cherry tomatoes before placing it in a steam-proof baking tray. Cook in the oven for 30 minutes, or until chicken is cooked through, or 165 degrees Fahrenheit (74 degrees Celsius). (4) Once cooked, top with feta cheese and lemon juice and set aside to cool. Keep heated before serving.

165. Greek Lemon Herb Chicken

Total Time: 50 minutes | Prep Time: 15 minutes

Ingredients:

4 bone-in, skin-on chicken thighs	2 tablespoons olive oil
1 teaspoon salt	½ teaspoon black pepper
1 teaspoon dried oregano	1 teaspoon dried thyme
½ teaspoon garlic powder	Zest and juice of 1 lemon
2 tablespoons fresh parsley, chopped	

Directions:

(1) Turn the steam oven's combined steam setting to 375°F (190°C), which is 40% steam and 60% convection. (2) Garlic powder, oregano, thyme, salt, black pepper, olive oil, lemon zest, and juice should be massaged into chicken thighs. (3) Position in a baking dish that can withstand steam, skin side up. (4) Preheat the oven to 175 degrees Fahrenheit (80 degrees Celsius) and bake for 40 minutes. (5) When ready to serve, take it out of the oven and top with chopped fresh parsley.

166. Moroccan Spiced Chickpeas

Total Time: 30 minutes | Prep Time: 10 minutes

Ingredients:

2 cups canned chickpeas, drained and rinsed	1 tablespoon olive oil
1 teaspoon ground cumin	1 teaspoon ground coriander
½ teaspoon smoked paprika	½ teaspoon ground cinnamon
¼ teaspoon cayenne pepper (optional)	2 garlic cloves, minced
1 small onion, finely chopped	½ cup diced tomatoes
½ teaspoon salt	¼ teaspoon black pepper
½ cup vegetable broth	

Directions:

(1) Set the steam oven to 375°F, or 190°C, with the combined steam and convection modes turned on. (2) In a pan that can endure steam, heat up a little olive oil. Add the garlic & continue cooking for 30 seconds after the

onion becomes transparent. (3) Add the cayenne, cinnamon, paprika, coriander, and cumin and mix well. Infuse with aroma and cook for 1 minute. (4) Put in the vegetable broth, chopped tomatoes, salt, pepper, and chickpeas. Mix thoroughly. (5) Place the pan in the steam oven and cook, stirring halfway through, for 20 minutes. (6) Accompany with hot rice or flatbread.

167. Mediterranean Quinoa and Vegetable Salad

Total Time: 25 minutes | Prep Time: 10 minutes

Ingredients:

1 cup quinoa, rinsed	2 cups water
½ cup cherry tomatoes, halved	½ cup cucumber, diced
¼ cup Kalamata olives, sliced	¼ cup red bell pepper, diced
¼ cup feta cheese, crumbled (optional)	2 tablespoons fresh parsley, chopped
2 tablespoons lemon juice	1 tablespoon olive oil
½ teaspoon salt	¼ teaspoon black pepper

Directions:

(1) With the steam-only setting, heat the steam oven to 212°F, or 100°C. (2) Put the quinoa and water in a dish that can withstand steam. Flutter the quinoa by steaming it for 15 minutes. (3) After the quinoa has cooled a little, move it to a big bowl. (4) Toss in some parsley, olives, bell pepper, tomatoes, cucumbers, and feta cheese (if using). (5) Lime juice, olive oil, salt, and pepper should be whisked together in a small basin. Toss the salad to blend after adding the drizzle. (6) Enjoy right away, or for a more flavorful experience, refrigerate for 30 minutes.

168. Roasted Sweet Potato and Black Bean Chili

Total Time: 40 minutes | Prep Time: 15 minutes

Ingredients:

2 medium sweet potatoes, peeled and diced	1 tablespoon olive oil
1 small onion, chopped	2 garlic cloves, minced
1 teaspoon ground cumin	1 teaspoon chili powder
½ teaspoon smoked paprika	½ teaspoon salt
¼ teaspoon black pepper	1 can black beans, drained & rinsed
1 (14 oz) can diced tomatoes	1 cup vegetable broth
½ cup corn kernels	¼ teaspoon red pepper flakes (optional)

Directions:

(1) Get the steam oven up to temperature in the combined steam mode, which uses 50% steam and 50% convection, at 400°F or 200°C. (2) Before placing the sweet potatoes on a baking pan that can withstand steam, toss them with the olive oil. Bake for fifteen minutes. (3) Prepare a steam-safe saucepan and sauté the garlic and onions until they are tender. Add the paprika, salt, black pepper, chili powder, and cumin and stir to combine. (4) Corn, chopped tomatoes, black beans, vegetable broth, and red pepper flakes should be added. Low heat for ten minutes. (5) Add the roasted sweet potatoes and simmer for another 5 minutes, stirring occasionally. (6) If

preferred, serve hot and sprinkle with fresh cilantro.

169. Creamy Spinach and Artichoke Dip

Total Time: 25 minutes | Prep Time: 10 minutes

Ingredients:

- 1 cup frozen spinach, thawed and drained
- 1 cup canned artichoke hearts, chopped
- ½ cup cream cheese, softened
- ½ cup Greek yogurt
- ½ cup shredded mozzarella cheese
- ¼ cup grated Parmesan cheese
- 1 garlic clove, minced
- ½ teaspoon onion powder
- ½ teaspoon salt
- ¼ teaspoon black pepper

Directions:

(1) Steam the oven to 375 degrees Fahrenheit (190 degrees Celsius) using 50% steam and 50% convection. (2) In a mixing bowl, combine artichokes, spinach, cream cheese, Greek yogurt, mozzarella, Parmesan, garlic, onion powder, salt, and black pepper. (3) After you've transferred the mixture to a baking dish that can withstand steam, be sure to layer it evenly. (4) If you want a bubbly, golden top, steam-bake it for 15 minutes. (5) Crackers, pita chips, or chopped vegetables go well with this warm dish.

170. Balsamic Glazed Chicken and Veggies

Total Time: 35 minutes | Prep Time: 10 minutes

Ingredients:

- 2 boneless, skinless chicken breasts
- 1 tablespoon olive oil
- 1 teaspoon Italian seasoning
- ½ teaspoon salt
- ¼ teaspoon black pepper
- 1 cup cherry tomatoes, halved
- 1 cup zucchini, sliced
- ½ red onion, sliced
- ¼ cup balsamic vinegar
- 1 tablespoon honey
- 1 teaspoon Dijon mustard

Directions:

(1) Set the steam oven to 375°F, or 190°C, with the combined steam and convection modes turned on. (2) Mix up the olive oil, Italian seasoning, salt, and black pepper in a bowl, then coat the chicken. (3) Preheat a steam-proof baking dish and add the chicken. Add zucchini, tomatoes, and red onion on both sides. (4) Combine the honey, Dijon mustard, & balsamic vinegar in a small bowl and whisk to combine. Finish by drizzling the chicken and vegetables. (5) Preheat a steam oven to 74 degrees Celsius (165 degrees Fahrenheit) and roast the chicken for 25 minutes or until done. (6) Set aside to cool for five minutes before slicing. Keep heated before serving.

171. Creamy Lemon Garlic Pasta

Total Time: 25 minutes | Prep Time: 10 minutes

Ingredients:

- 8 oz fettuccine or linguine
- 1 ½ cups heavy cream
- 3 cloves garlic, minced
- Zest and juice of 1 lemon

½ cup grated Parmesan cheese	2 tbsp butter
½ tsp salt	¼ tsp black pepper
½ tsp red pepper flakes (optional)	2 tbsp chopped fresh parsley

Directions:

(1) Bring the steam oven up to temperature, then set it to 212°F or 100°C. (2) Fill a baking dish that can withstand steam with water and add the pasta. To get an al dente texture, steam for 10 to 12 minutes. Reserve the drained liquid. (3) Melt the butter in a separate steam-safe dish and add the garlic, lemon zest, and heavy cream. To get it warm, steam it for 5 minutes. (4) When done baking, take the pan out and mix in the Parmesan, lemon juice, salt, and pepper. (5) Return the pasta to the steam oven for three more minutes to let the sauce and pasta combine. (6) Serve heated with a sprinkle of parsley for garnish.

172. Creamy Avocado Pasta

Total Time: 20 minutes | Prep Time: 10 minutes

Ingredients:

8 oz spaghetti or fettuccine	1 ripe avocado, peeled and pitted
½ cup Greek yogurt	2 tbsp olive oil
2 cloves garlic, minced	Juice of 1 lime
¼ tsp salt	¼ tsp black pepper
½ tsp red pepper flakes (optional)	¼ cup grated Parmesan cheese
Fresh basil leaves for garnish	

Directions:

(1) Bring the steam oven up to temperature, then set it to 212°F or 100°C. (2) Add enough water to a steam-safe dish to cover the pasta. To get an al dente texture, steam for 10 to 12 minutes. Reserve the drained liquid. (3) Throw in some garlic, lime juice, olive oil, Greek yogurt, avocado, salt, and black pepper, and mix it all together. Puree the mixture. (4) After cooking the pasta, toss it with the avocado sauce. Transfer to a steam-safe dish and simmer for 3 minutes or until heated through. (5) Add some fresh basil and Parmesan cheese as a garnish. Serve right away.

173. Balsamic Glazed Roasted Potatoes

Total Time: 40 minutes | Prep Time: 10 minutes

Ingredients:

1 ½ lbs baby potatoes, halved	3 tbsp olive oil
2 tbsp balsamic vinegar	1 tsp garlic powder
½ tsp salt	½ tsp black pepper
1 tsp dried thyme	¼ tsp red pepper flakes (optional)

Directions:

(1) Turn the convection steam oven up to 400 degrees Fahrenheit (200 degrees Celsius). (2) Olive oil, balsamic vinegar, garlic powder, salt, pepper, thyme, and red pepper flakes should be mixed with the potatoes in a big basin. (3) Lay down the potatoes in a single layer on a baking sheet that can withstand steam. Cook, stirring once, for 25 to 30 minutes. (4) Serve warm after taking out of the oven.

174. Balsamic Chicken and Vegetables

Total Time: 35 minutes | Prep Time: 10 minutes

Ingredients:

2 boneless, skinless chicken breasts	1 zucchini, sliced
1 red bell pepper, sliced	½ red onion, sliced
3 tbsp balsamic vinegar	2 tbsp olive oil
2 cloves garlic, minced	1 tsp dried oregano
½ tsp salt	½ tsp black pepper

Directions:

(1) Switch to combined steam mode and heat the steam oven to 375°F, or 190°C. (2) Combine olive oil, garlic, oregano, salt, and pepper with balsamic vinegar in a basin. (3) Spread half of the balsamic mixture over the chicken breasts in a baking dish that can withstand steam. (4) In a separate bowl, marge the bell pepper, onion, zucchini, and the rest of the balsamic vinegar. (5) Cook the chicken until it reaches 75°C, which should take around 25 minutes, in the steam oven with the other food. (6) Arrange the roasted veggies on a platter and top with sliced chicken.

175. Balsamic Roasted Brussels Sprouts with Bacon

Total Time: 35 minutes | Prep Time: 10 minutes

Ingredients:

1 lb Brussels sprouts, halved	4 slices bacon, chopped
2 tbsp balsamic vinegar	1 tbsp olive oil
½ tsp salt	¼ tsp black pepper

Directions:

(1) Turn the steam oven's combined steam setting to 400°F (200°C). (2) The Brussels sprouts should be mixed in a basin with the balsamic vinegar, salt, pepper, olive oil, and everything. (3) Arrange the bacon and Brussels sprouts in a steam-safe baking dish. (4) To get a caramelized finish, roast for 25-30 minutes, tossing halfway through. (5) Enjoy when hot.

176. Lemon Herb Roasted Potatoes

Total Time: 40 minutes | Prep Time: 10 minutes

Ingredients:

1 ½ lbs baby potatoes, halved	2 tbsp olive oil
1 tbsp lemon juice	1 tsp lemon zest
1 tsp dried oregano	½ tsp dried thyme
½ tsp garlic powder	Salt and pepper, to taste
2 tbsp fresh parsley, chopped	

Directions:

(1) Turn the steam oven's combo steam-roast setting to 400°F (200°C). (2) Olive oil, lemon zest and juice, oregano, thyme, garlic powder, salt, & pepper should be mixed with the potatoes in a big basin. (3) Evenly distribute the potatoes on a steam oven pan with perforations. (4) After 30 minutes of roasting, shake the tray halfway through to ensure even browning and tenderness of the potatoes. (5) Garnish each serving with a little fresh parsley.

177. Lemon Garlic Herb Chicken Thighs

Total Time: 50 minutes | Prep Time: 10 minutes

Ingredients:

4 bone-in, skin-on chicken thighs	2 tbsp olive oil
2 tbsp lemon juice	1 tbsp lemon zest
3 cloves garlic, minced	1 tsp dried oregano
½ tsp dried rosemary	½ tsp salt
½ tsp black pepper	1 tbsp fresh parsley, chopped

Directions:

(1) Turn the steam oven's combined steam-roast setting to 375°F, which is 190°C. (2) Marge the olive oil, lemon zest & juice, garlic, oregano, rosemary, salt, & pepper in a bowl. (3) After 10 minutes of rubbing in the marinade, the chicken thighs are ready to cook. (4) On a steam oven sheet with holes in it, lay the chicken thighs. (5) Roast for about 40 minutes, or until the outside is golden brown & the inside at a temperature of 75 °C. Serve heated with a sprinkle of fresh parsley for garnish.

178. Teriyaki Chicken Thighs

Total Time: 45 minutes | Prep Time: 10 minutes

Ingredients:

4 bone-in, skin-on chicken thighs	¼ cup soy sauce
2 tbsp honey	1 tbsp rice vinegar
1 tbsp sesame oil	2 cloves garlic, minced
1 tsp grated ginger	½ tsp black pepper
1 tsp cornstarch (optional for thickening)	1 tbsp sesame seeds, for garnish
1 green onion, sliced	

Directions:

(1) Bring the steam oven up to temperature on the steam-roast combo setting, which is 375°F or 190°C. (2) To make the sauce, marinate the soy sauce, honey, rice vinegar, sesame oil, ginger, garlic, and black pepper in a mixer bowl. (3) For a minimum of ten minutes, let the chicken marinate in the sauce. (4) Roast, basting halfway through, the chicken thighs for 35 minutes on a steam oven pan with holes punched into it. (5) In a small saucepan over medium heat, thicken the leftover marinade with cornstarch if you want. (6) After the sauce has thickened, pour it over the chicken. Top with green onions and sesame seeds.

179. Greek Stuffed Eggplant

Total Time: 50 minutes | Prep Time: 15 minutes

Ingredients:

2 medium eggplants, halved lengthwise	1 tbsp olive oil
½ lb ground lamb or beef	½ onion, diced
2 cloves garlic, minced	1 tomato, diced
½ tsp dried oregano	½ tsp ground cinnamon
Salt and pepper, to taste	¼ cup crumbled feta cheese
1 tbsp fresh parsley, chopped	

Directions:

(1) Turn the steam oven's combined steam-bake setting to 375°F (190°C) for preheating. (2) Leave a ¼-inch margin while scooping out the eggplant flesh. Before setting aside, mince the meat. (3) Melt the olive oil in a skillet set

over medium heat. After the garlic and onions have softened, add the ground beef & continue cooking until it becomes brown. (4) Mix in the tomatoes, oregano, cinnamon, salt, and pepper, along with the diced eggplant flesh. Allow to cook for a duration of 5 minutes. (5) Spoon the filling into the eggplant halves & set them in a baking tray. (6) 30 minutes in a steam oven. After another 5 minutes in the oven, top with the feta cheese. (7) Lastly, serve with a sprinkle of fresh parsley.

180. Quinoa-Stuffed Zucchini Boats

Total Time: 40 minutes | Prep Time: 10 minutes

Ingredients:

3 medium zucchinis, halved lengthwise	½ cup cooked quinoa
1 tbsp olive oil	½ onion, diced
1 clove garlic, minced	½ cup cherry tomatoes, diced
¼ cup black olives, chopped	¼ tsp dried basil
¼ tsp dried oregano	Salt and pepper, to taste
¼ cup shredded mozzarella cheese (optional)	1 tbsp fresh basil, chopped

Directions:

(1) Turn the steam oven's combined steam-bake setting to 375°F (190°C) for preheating. (2) Extract the zucchini flesh, being sure to leave a border of half an inch. Before setting aside, mince the meat. (3) In a saucepan, hot the olive oil over middle heat. Soften the garlic and onions by sautéing them. Toss in some salt, pepper, diced zucchini, cherry tomatoes, black olives, basil, and oregano. Allow to cook for a duration of 5 minutes. (4) Before turning off the stove, mix in the cooked quinoa. (5) Arrange the filled zucchini shells on a steam oven plate with perforations. (6) Steam bake for twenty-five minutes. Finish baking for five more minutes if mozzarella is used. (7) Add some fresh basil as a garnish just before serving.

181. Sweet and Spicy Chicken Stir-Fry

Total Time: 30 minutes | Prep Time: 10 minutes

Ingredients:

Thickly cut, boneless, skinless chicken breast, 1 pound	1 red bell pepper, sliced
1 yellow bell pepper, sliced	1 cup snap peas
1 small onion, sliced	2 cloves garlic, minced
1-inch piece ginger, grated	2 tbsp soy sauce
1 tbsp honey	1 tsp sriracha (adjust to taste)
Two tablespoons of water & 1 tablespoon of cornstarch	1 tbsp sesame oil
1 tbsp olive oil	1 tsp sesame seeds (for garnish)
Green onions, sliced (for garnish)	

Directions:

(1) Set the steam oven to combination steam and heat it to 210°F, or 100°C. (2) Combine the honey, sriracha, and soy sauce and let them marinate the chicken. Give it a five-minute rest. (3) A pan that may be used in a steam oven is ideal for heating olive oil. Sauté for 1 minute after adding ginger and garlic. (4) Cook,

stirring periodically, for five minutes after adding the chicken. (5) Add the onion, snap peas, bell peppers, and toss well. Continue steam-cooking for a further five to seven minutes. (6) Mix in the sesame oil and cornstarch slurry. Continue cooking for another 2 minutes or until the mixture thickens. (7) Serve topped with green onions & sesame seeds. Top with cooked noodles or rice.

182. Thai Red Curry Beef

Total Time: 40 minutes | Prep Time: 15 minutes

Ingredients:

- 1 lb (450g) beef sirloin, thinly sliced
- 1 can (13.5 oz) coconut milk
- 2 tbsp Thai red curry paste
- 1 cup broccoli florets
- 1 red bell pepper, sliced
- 1 small zucchini, sliced
- 1 small onion, diced
- 2 cloves garlic, minced
- 1 tbsp fish sauce
- 1 tbsp brown sugar
- 1 tsp lime zest
- 1 tbsp olive oil
- Fresh basil leaves for garnish

Directions:

(1) On steam mode, bring the steam oven up to 212°F, or 100°C. (2) A pan that may be used in a steam oven is ideal for heating olive oil. Red curry paste, garlic, and onion should be sautéed for one or two minutes. (3) While stirring periodically, cook the meat for three minutes. (4) Add lime zest, brown sugar, fish sauce, coconut milk, and a splash of aquarium sauce. Blend well. (5) Toss in some zucchini, bell pepper, and broccoli. When the beef reaches the desired doneness, steam it for around fifteen to twenty minutes. (6) Serve over jasmine rice & top with fresh basil.

183. Lemon Garlic Chicken Thighs

Total Time: 45 minutes | Prep Time: 10 minutes

Ingredients:

- 4 bone-in, skin-on chicken thighs
- 2 tbsp olive oil
- 3 cloves garlic, minced
- 1 lemon, zested and juiced
- 1 tsp dried oregano
- ½ tsp paprika
- Salt and black pepper to taste
- 1 cup cherry tomatoes, halved
- ½ cup chicken broth
- Fresh parsley for garnish

Directions:

(1) Switch to combined steam mode and heat the steam oven to 375°F, or 190°C. (2) Oregano, paprika, garlic, lemon zest, lemon juice, olive oil, and pepper should be sprinkled over the chicken. (3) Arrange the chicken thighs and skin side up in a pan that is suitable for use in a steam oven. (4) Cherry tomatoes and chicken broth should be added after roasting for 25 minutes. (5) When the chicken gets to a golden color and an internal heat of 75°C, turn off the heat. (6) Parsley is a nice garnish, and you can serve it with rice or steamed veggies.

184. Mediterranean Stuffed Peppers

Total Time: 50 minutes | Prep Time: 15 minutes

Ingredients:

- 4 large bell peppers (any color)
- 1 cup cooked quinoa

1 cup canned chickpeas, drained and rinsed	½ cup cherry tomatoes, diced
¼ cup black olives, chopped	½ cup feta cheese, crumbled
1 tsp dried oregano	1 tsp garlic powder
Salt and black pepper to taste	2 tbsp olive oil
½ cup vegetable broth	

Directions:

(1) Set the steam oven's combined steam setting to 350°F (175°C) for preheating. (2) Remove the seeds and tops from the bell peppers. (3) In a bowl, combine the quinoa, chickpeas, olives, feta, oregano, garlic powder, salt, and olive oil. Add the cherry tomatoes and olives. (4) Fill the peppers with the quinoa filling and set them on a dish that may be steam-oven-safe. (5) Cook in a steam oven for 30–35 minutes after adding vegetable broth. (6) Warm it up and top it with fresh herbs if you want.

185. Creamy Avocado Chicken and Veggies

Total Time: 35 minutes | Prep Time: 10 minutes

Ingredients:

2 boneless, skinless chicken breasts	1 avocado, mashed
½ cup Greek yogurt	1 tbsp lemon juice
1 tsp garlic powder	1 cup asparagus spears, trimmed
1 cup zucchini, sliced	1 small red bell pepper, sliced
Salt and black pepper to taste	1 tbsp olive oil

Directions:

(1) In combination steam mode, bring the steam oven up to 210°F or 100°C. (2) Rub garlic powder, black pepper, and salt into chicken breasts. (3) Coat the chicken with cooking spray and roast it in a steam oven for 20 minutes. (4) Toss in some bell peppers, zucchini, and asparagus. Add an additional 10 minutes of steaming time. (5) In a bowl, combine the pitted avocado, Greek yogurt, and squeezed lemon juice. (6) Place the chicken and vegetables on a platter and drizzle with the rich avocado sauce.

186. Thai Spiced Pork Tenderloin

Total Time: 45 minutes | Prep Time: 15 minutes

Ingredients:

1 pork tenderloin (about 1 lb)	2 tbsp soy sauce
1 tbsp fish sauce	1 tbsp honey
1 tbsp lime juice	2 garlic cloves, minced
1 tsp ground coriander	1 tsp ground cumin
1 tsp chili powder	1/2 tsp turmeric
Salt and pepper, to taste	Fresh cilantro, chopped (for garnish)

Directions:

(1) Turn the steam oven on high heat (400°F). (2) Combine the spices, garlic, lime juice, honey, fish sauce, & soy sauce in a small bowl. (3) Pork tenderloin should be rubbed with the marinade. (4) After 30 minutes of steaming, or until the internal temperature reaches 145°F, transfer the tenderloin to the steam oven. (5) Take out of the steam oven and set aside to rest

for five minutes. (6) Add a little of fresh cilantro as a garnish before serving.

187. Honey Glazed Salmon

Total Time: 20 minutes | Prep Time: 5 minutes

Ingredients:

- 4 salmon fillets (6 oz each)
- 1 tbsp Dijon mustard
- 1 tsp soy sauce
- Fresh parsley, chopped (for garnish)
- 2 tbsp honey
- 1 tbsp lemon juice
- Salt and pepper, to taste

Directions:

(1) Get the steam oven hot and ready at 375°F. (2) Combine the honey, Dijon mustard, lemon juice, soy sauce, salt, & pepper in a small bowl and whisk or stir. (3) Transfer the fillets of salmon to the steam oven pan and coat them with the honey glaze. (4) Sauté the salmon for ten to twelve minutes or until it reaches the desired doneness. (5) Add some fresh parsley as a garnish just before serving.

188. Garlic Butter Chicken Thighs

Total Time: 40 minutes | Prep Time: 10 minutes

Ingredients:

- 4 bone-in, skin-on chicken thighs
- 4 garlic cloves, minced
- 1 tsp dried thyme
- 3 tbsp unsalted butter, melted
- 1 tbsp lemon juice
- Salt and pepper, to taste
- Fresh parsley, chopped (for garnish)

Directions:

(1) Turn the steam oven on high heat (375°F). (2) Put the garlic, lemon juice, thyme, salt, & pepper in a bowl & stir until combined. (3) Distribute the garlic butter mixture evenly over the chicken thighs. (4) Lay the skin-side-up chicken thighs on the steam oven pan. (5) To get a chicken's internal temperature of 165 degrees Fahrenheit, steam it for 30 to 35 minutes. (6) Lastly, serve with a sprinkle of fresh parsley.

189. Greek Chicken and Couscous Salad

Total Time: 30 minutes | Prep Time: 10 minutes

Ingredients:

- 2 boneless, skinless chicken breasts
- 1 cucumber, diced
- 1/2 red onion, thinly sliced
- 1/4 cup feta cheese, crumbled
- 2 tbsp lemon juice
- Salt and pepper, to taste
- 1 cup couscous
- 1 cup cherry tomatoes, halved
- 1/4 cup kalamata olives, pitted & sliced
- 1 tbsp olive oil
- 1 tsp dried oregano

Directions:

(1) Turn the steam oven on high heat (375°F). (2) Pepper, salt, and dried oregano are the seasonings you need for chicken breasts. (3) After 20 to 25 minutes of steaming, the chicken should have an internal heat of 165 degrees Fahrenheit. (4) In the meantime, cook the

couscous as directed on the box. (5) Toss the couscous, cucumber, tomatoes, onion, olives, and feta in a big bowl. (6) Before tossing the chicken with the salad, slice it. Olive oil & lemon juice should be drizzled over. (7) After a good toss, serve.

190. Chicken and Vegetable Kabobs

Total Time: 35 minutes | Prep Time: 15 minutes

Ingredients:

- 2 chicken breasts (without bones & skin) diced into 1-inch pieces
- 1 zucchini, cut into thick slices
- 1 tbsp olive oil
- 1 tsp garlic powder
- 1 red bell pepper, cut into chunks
- 1 yellow onion, cut into chunks
- 1 tsp paprika
- Salt and pepper, to taste
- Wooden skewers that have been immersed in water for half an hour

Directions:

(1) A steam oven should be preheated to 375°F. (2) Olive oil, paprika, garlic powder, salt, & pepper should be mixed with the veggies and chicken in a dish. (3) Alternate threading the skewers with the veggies and meat. (4) Cook the chicken for 25-30 minutes, or until skewers are tender, on a steam oven tray. (5) Warm up and savor!

191. Roasted Vegetable Medley

Total Time: 35 minutes | Prep Time: 10 minutes

Ingredients:

- 2 cups broccoli florets
- 1 cup cherry tomatoes
- 1 zucchini, sliced
- 1 tsp garlic powder
- Salt and pepper to taste
- 2 cups diced butternut squash
- 1 red bell pepper, sliced
- 3 tbsp olive oil
- 1 tsp dried thyme

Directions:

(1) Steam ovens should be preheated to 400°F or 200°C. (2) Combine the veggies with the olive oil, garlic powder, thyme, salt, and pepper in a big basin and mix to coat. (3) Arrange the veggies in a uniform layer on a baking sheet. (4) After 20 to 25 minutes of roasting in the steam oven, stir halfway through to get a little caramelized and soft texture. (5) Warm it up and enjoy it as a main course or a side dish.

192. Honey Mustard Brussels Sprouts

Total Time: 30 minutes | Prep Time: 10 minutes

Ingredients:

- 1 lb Brussels sprouts, halved
- 2 tbsp Dijon mustard
- 1 tsp apple cider vinegar
- 3 tbsp olive oil
- 1 tbsp honey
- Salt and pepper to taste

Directions:

(1) A steam oven should be preheated to 375°F, or 190°C. (2) Combine the olive oil, Dijon mustard, honey, vinegar, salt, & pepper in a bowl & whisk to combine. (3) Mix the honey mustard with the Brussels sprouts and toss to coat. (4) Make sure there's just one layer of

Brussels sprouts on the baking sheet. (5) Caramelize and soften in the oven for 20 minutes, tossing halfway through. (6) This dish is perfect for serving as a side.

193. Thai Spiced Roasted Chicken

Total Time: 1 hour 10 minutes | Prep Time: 15 minutes

Ingredients:

- 1 whole chicken (3-4 lbs)
- 1 tbsp coconut milk
- 1 tsp lime juice
- Salt and pepper to taste
- 2 tbsp red Thai curry paste
- 2 tbsp olive oil
- 1 tsp fish sauce

Directions:

(1) A steam oven should be preheated to 375°F, or 190°C. (2) Combine the coconut milk, curry paste, sea salt, pepper, lime juice, olive oil, and fish sauce in a small bowl. (3) Spread the marinade over the chicken, being sure to get beneath the skin as well. (4) Before placing the chicken in the steam oven, set it on a roasting rack. (5) Cook, turning once halfway through, until the thermometer reads 165 degrees Fahrenheit (74 degrees Celsius). (6) Ten minutes should pass before cutting the bird. Accompany with steaming veggies or rice.

194. Pesto Chicken and Vegetables

Total Time: 40 minutes | Prep Time: 10 minutes

Ingredients:

- 4 boneless, skinless chicken breasts
- 2 cups cherry tomatoes
- 1 cup green beans, trimmed
- 1/2 cup pesto sauce
- Salt and pepper to taste
- 1 zucchini, sliced
- 2 tbsp olive oil

Directions:

(1) Steam oven temperature should be set at 375°F or 190°C. (2) Season chicken breasts with salt & pepper & rub with olive oil. Arrange them in a baking dish. (3) Add the olive oil, salt, & pepper to the veggies in another bowl. Incorporate them into the chicken's skin. (4) Spoon some pesto sauce on top of each chicken breast. (5) Keep roasting until the bird achieves an internal temperature of 74°C (165°F), which should take around 25-30 minutes. (6) If you like, you may serve it hot and top it with some fresh basil.

195. Roasted Garlic Mashed Cauliflower

Total Time: 25 minutes | Prep Time: 10 minutes

Ingredients:

- One large head of cauliflower, cut into florets
- 2 tbsp butter or olive oil
- Salt and pepper to taste
- 4 cloves roasted garlic
- One-fourth cup heavy cream (or milk if you want a lighter mixture)
- Fresh parsley for garnish (optional)

Directions:

(1) Steam oven temperature should be set at 375°F or 190°C. (2) To make the cauliflower florets soft, bake them in a steamer for 10 to 12 minutes. (3) After the cauliflower has cooked, place it in a food processor. Whisk in the

roasted garlic, butter, cream, salt, and pepper. (4) Whisk or mix until combined. If needed, adjust the seasoning. (5) Warm it up and top it with fresh parsley if you want.

196. Lemon Garlic Brussels Sprouts

Total Time: 25 minutes | Prep Time: 10 minutes

Ingredients:

1 lb (450 g) Brussels sprouts, trimmed and halved	2 tbsp olive oil
2 cloves garlic, minced	Juice and zest of 1 lemon
1 tsp salt	½ tsp black pepper

Directions:

(1) Set the steam oven to a temperature of 400°F, or 200°C, using the convection and steam combo setting. (2) The Brussels sprouts should be mixed in a big basin with garlic, lemon zest, olive oil, salt, and pepper. (3) Evenly distribute the sprouts on a baking sheet with holes punched into it or a steam oven tray. (4) Cook, turning once, for 20 minutes or until soft and browned. (5) Serve immediately after drizzling with lemon juice.

197. Roasted Red Pepper Hummus

Total Time: 20 minutes | Prep Time: 10 minutes

Ingredients:

2 large red bell peppers, halved & seeded	1 can (15 oz/425 g) chickpeas, drained and rinsed
3 tbsp tahini	2 cloves garlic, minced
Juice of 1 lemon	3 tbsp olive oil
1 tsp cumin	½ tsp smoked paprika
Salt and pepper to taste	

Directions:

(1) Get the steam oven preheated to 375°F, or 190°C, using the convection setting. (2) Red bell peppers, cut side down, should be roasted in a steam oven for 12–15 minutes or until the skin blisters and becomes a little black. After allowing them to cool, remove the skins. (3) Marge all the ingredients in a blender or food processor & puree until smooth. Add the roasted red peppers, chickpeas, tahini, garlic, lemon juice, olive oil, cumin, smoked paprika, salt, and pepper. Blend until completely smooth, adding more water as needed to get the desired consistency. (4) Enjoy with pita bread or a side of veggies.

198. Greek Chicken and Quinoa Bowl

Total Time: 35 minutes | Prep Time: 15 minutes

Ingredients:

2 chicken breasts, boneless and skinless	1 cup quinoa
1 ¾ cups water or chicken stock	1 tbsp olive oil
1 tsp dried oregano	Juice of 1 lemon
1 cucumber, diced	1 cup cherry tomatoes, halved
½ cup Kalamata olives, sliced	¼ cup feta cheese, crumbled
Salt and pepper to taste	

Directions:

(1) Get the steam and convection oven up to temperature, then set it to 400°F or 200°C. (2) Before sprinkling olive oil on top, rub the chicken breasts with a seasoning blend of oregano, lemon juice, salt, & pepper. To ensure they are cooked through, steam-roast them for 20 to 25 minutes on a perforated tray. (3) At the same time, run cold water over the quinoa to rinse it. To make the quinoa soft and absorb the liquid, place it in a steam oven-safe dish and cook it at 212°F (100°C) on steam-only mode for 18-20 minutes. You may use water or stock as a substitute for water. (4) Set up the basin: Assemble the quinoa in a layer with the chopped cucumber, cherry tomatoes, olives, and sliced chicken. Scatter crumbled feta on top. (5) Enjoy either heated or cooled.

199. Honey Soy Glazed Pork

Total Time: 40 minutes | Prep Time: 10 minutes

Ingredients:

4 boneless pork chops	3 tbsp soy sauce
2 tbsp honey	1 tbsp rice vinegar
1 tsp sesame oil	2 cloves garlic, minced
1 tsp grated ginger	1 tbsp sesame seeds
2 green onions, sliced	

Directions:

(1) Gather all the ingredients in a small bowl and whisk them together. Add the rice vinegar, soy sauce, ginger, garlic, sesame oil, & honey. Coat the pork chops with the marinade & set them in a shallow dish. Marinate them for fifteen to twenty minutes. (2) Set the steam oven to a preheated temperature of 375°F, or 190°C, using the steam and convection combo setting. (3) Arrange the pork chops in a steam oven dish and coat them with the marinade. After 25 minutes of cooking, flip the pork over to ensure even cooking. (4) Sesame seeds and green onions make a lovely garnish.

200. Roasted Cauliflower and Chickpea Salad

Total Time: 30 minutes | Prep Time: 10 minutes

Ingredients:

1 medium head cauliflower, cut into florets	1 can 425 g chickpeas, drained & rinsed
3 tbsp olive oil	1 tsp ground cumin
½ tsp smoked paprika	Salt and pepper to taste
2 cups arugula or spinach	¼ cup parsley, chopped
Juice of 1 lemon	

Directions:

(1) Set the steam oven to a temperature of 400°F, or 200°C, using the convection and steam combo setting. (2) Before tossing the chickpeas and cauliflower florets with the chickpeas, add the cumin, smoked paprika, vinegar, salt, and pepper. Evenly distribute them on a steam oven baking sheet. (3) Cauliflower should be roasted for twenty to twenty-five minutes, turning once halfway through or until it becomes soft and golden. (4) Toss the roasted chickpeas and cauliflower with the arugula, parsley, and lemon juice when they have cooled a little. (5) You may eat it warm as a salad or cold.

201. Sweet and Spicy Salmon

Total Time: 25 minutes | Prep Time: 10 minutes

Ingredients:

- 4 salmon fillets (about 6 oz each)
- 2 tbsp soy sauce
- 1 tsp garlic powder
- 1 tbsp olive oil
- Lemon wedges for serving
- 3 tbsp honey
- 1 tbsp sriracha (adjust to taste)
- 1 tsp smoked paprika
- Salt and pepper to taste

Directions:

(1) A steam oven should be preheated to 400°F or 200°C. (2) Combine the honey, soy sauce, sriracha, garlic powder, smoked paprika, & olive oil in a small bowl and whisk to combine. (3) Before seasoning with salt and pepper, pat dry the salmon fillets. (4) Lay parchment paper-lined steam oven trays with the salmon on top. Apply a large amount of sauce to coat each fillet. (5) Cook the salmon in a steam oven for 12–15 minutes or until it flakes readily when tested with a fork. (6) Add some lemon wedges for garnish and savor!

202. Baked Honey Mustard Chicken

Total Time: 35 minutes | Prep Time: 10 minutes

Ingredients:

- 4 boneless, skinless chicken breasts
- 1/3 cup Dijon mustard
- 3 tbsp honey
- 1 tsp dried thyme
- Fresh parsley, chopped (for garnish)
- 2 cloves garlic, minced
- Salt and pepper to taste

Directions:

(1) Before using, bring the steam oven up to a temperature of 190°C. (2) Combine the remaining ingredients in a bowl: honey, chopped garlic, dry thyme, Dijon mustard, salt, and pepper. (3) Evenly coat the chicken breasts with the honey mustard mixture and set them on a steam oven tray. (4) When the chicken reaches an internal heat of 74°C, remove it from the steam oven and let it rest for 25-30 minutes. (5) Serve with a sprinkle of minced parsley for garnish.

203. Lemon Herb Roasted Brussels Sprouts

Total Time: 30 minutes | Prep Time: 10 minutes

Ingredients:

- 1 lb Brussels sprouts, trimmed and halved
- 1 tbsp lemon juice
- 1 tsp dried rosemary
- Salt and pepper to taste
- 2 tbsp olive oil
- 1 tsp lemon zest
- 1 tsp dried thyme

Directions:

(1) Steam oven temperature should be set at 400°F or 200°C. (2) Sal, pepper, rosemary, lemon zest, olive oil, and Brussels sprouts should be mixed together. (3) A steam oven plate should be lined with evenly spread Brussels sprouts. (4) To get a golden brown crust and soft inside, steam-roast for 20 to 25

minutes, stirring once halfway through. (5) Warm up and serve as a complement.

204. Balsamic Glazed Chicken

Total Time: 30 minutes | Prep Time: 10 minutes

Ingredients:

- 4 boneless, skinless chicken thighs
- 2 tbsp brown sugar
- 2 cloves garlic, minced
- Salt and pepper to taste
- 1/4 cup balsamic vinegar
- 2 tbsp olive oil
- 1 tsp dried oregano

Directions:

(1) Before using, bring the steam oven up to a heat of 190°C. (2) The balsamic vinegar, brown sugar, olive oil, minced garlic, oregano, salt, and pepper should all be whisked together in a bowl. (3) After seasoning the chicken thighs, spray them with the balsamic mixture and set them on a steam oven tray. (4) When the chicken reaches an internal heat of 74°C, remove it from the steam oven and let it rest for 25-30 minutes. (5) Accompany with your preferred accompaniment and savor.

205. Garlic Butter Mushrooms

Total Time: 20 minutes | Prep Time: 5 minutes

Ingredients:

- 1 lb button mushrooms, cleaned and trimmed
- 2 cloves garlic, minced
- 3 tbsp unsalted butter, melted
- 1 tsp dried parsley
- Salt and pepper to taste

Directions:

(1) A steam oven should be preheated to 375°F, or 190°C. (2) Combine the sliced mushrooms with the melted butter, salt, pepper, parsley, and chopped garlic in a mixing bowl. (3) Evenly distribute the mushrooms on a steam oven baking sheet. (4) To get soft, golden mushrooms, steam-bake for 15 to 20 minutes, stirring once halfway through. (5) Warm it up and serve it as an appetizer or side dish.

206. Creamy Tomato Basil Soup

Total Time: 30 minutes | Prep Time: 10 minutes

Ingredients:

- 2 lbs ripe tomatoes, quartered
- 3 garlic cloves, minced
- 1 cup vegetable broth
- 1 tsp sugar (optional)
- 1/4 cup fresh basil leaves, chopped
- 1 medium onion, diced
- 2 tbsp olive oil
- 1 cup heavy cream
- Salt and black pepper, to taste

Directions:

(1) Turn the steam oven's temperature up to 212 degrees Fahrenheit (100 degrees Celsius). (2) On a steam-safe plate, combine the tomatoes, garlic, onion, and olive oil. Cook on high heat for a duration of 20 minutes. (3) After the mixture has steamed, pour it into a blender along with the vegetable broth. Process until smooth. (4) In a saucepan, combine the soup with the heavy cream; add salt, pepper, and sugar to taste. (5) Incorporate the fresh basil

just before serving, & if necessary, reheat slowly over low heat.

207. Thai Coconut Chicken and Vegetable Curry

Total Time: 40 minutes | Prep Time: 15 minutes

Ingredients:

- 1 lb chicken breast, diced
- 1 zucchini, sliced
- 2 tbsp red curry paste
- 1 tbsp fish sauce
- 2 tbsp lime juice
- 1 red bell pepper, sliced
- 1 cup broccoli florets
- 1 can (13.5 oz) coconut milk
- 1 tsp sugar
- 1/4 cup fresh cilantro, chopped

Directions:

(1) Turn the steam oven's temperature up to 212 degrees Fahrenheit (100 degrees Celsius). (2) Skewer the broccoli, bell pepper, zucchini, and chicken on a steam-safe platter. Ten minutes of steaming is all it takes. (3) Toss the curry paste, coconut milk, fish sauce, sugar, and lime juice into a skillet and cook over medium heat, stirring occasionally. (4) Simmer the chicken and veggies in the sauce for 5 minutes after steaming. (5) Top with chopped cilantro and serve hot.

208. Herb-crusted pork Tenderloin

Total Time: 40 minutes | Prep Time: 10 minutes

Ingredients:

- 1 lb pork tenderloin
- 1/4 cup breadcrumbs
- 2 tbsp Dijon mustard
- 2 tbsp fresh parsley, chopped
- 1 tbsp fresh thyme leaves
- Salt and black pepper, to taste
- 1 tbsp olive oil

Directions:

(1) Set the steam and convection oven to 356°F, or 180°C, for preheating. (2) After coating the pork tenderloin with Dijon mustard, proceed to press the breadcrumb mixture (which includes breadcrumbs, parsley, thyme, olive oil, salt, and pepper) over its surface. (3) Steak should be cooked for 30 minutes, or until internal temperature reaches 145°F, or 63°C, in a steam-safe pan. (4) Five minutes should pass before chopping the meat. Warm it up before plating.

209. Spinach and Ricotta Stuffed Chicken

Total Time: 35 minutes | Prep Time: 15 minutes

Ingredients:

- 4 boneless chicken breasts
- 1/2 cup ricotta cheese
- 1 tsp garlic powder
- 1 tbsp olive oil
- 1 cup fresh spinach, chopped
- 1/4 cup grated Parmesan cheese
- Salt and black pepper, to taste

Directions:

(1) Set the steam and convection oven to 356°F, or 180°C, for preheating. (2) Toss together the spinach, ricotta, Parmesan, garlic powder, salt, and pepper in a vessel. (3) Spoon the spinach-ricotta filling into each chicken breast that you've cut. (4) After brushing the chicken with olive oil, set it on a steam-safe plate. Bring the temperature inside to 165 degrees Fahrenheit (74 degrees Celsius) by

baking for 25 to 30 minutes. (5) Steamed veggies or a side salad are good accompaniments.

210. Lemon Butter Roasted Salmon

Total Time: 25 minutes | Prep Time: 5 minutes

Ingredients:

4 salmon fillets (6 oz each)	2 tbsp unsalted butter, melted
2 tbsp lemon juice	1 tsp lemon zest
1 tbsp fresh dill, chopped	Salt and black pepper, to taste

Directions:

(1) Get the steam oven ready by setting it to 356°F, or 180°C, using the steam and convection function. (2) On a steam-safe plate, arrange the salmon fillets. Melt some butter and brush it over, then sprinkle some lemon juice on top. (3) After seasoning the fillets with salt & pepper, top with lemon zest and dill. (4) When tested with a fork, cooked salmon should flake readily after 15 to 20 minutes in the oven. (5) Top with rice or steamed asparagus and serve hot.

211. Stuffed Portobello Mushrooms

Total Time: 35 minutes | Prep Time: 15 minutes

Ingredients:

4 large Portobello mushrooms	1 cup cooked quinoa
½ cup grated Parmesan cheese	½ cup chopped spinach
¼ cup breadcrumbs	2 cloves garlic, minced
1 tsp olive oil	Salt and pepper to taste

Directions:

(1) Make sure the steam oven is heated up to 350°F (175°C). (2) After cleaning the Portobello mushrooms, cut off their stems and remove their gills. Dip the tops of the caps into olive oil and put down. (3) The cooked quinoa, Parmesan cheese, spinach, breadcrumbs, garlic, salt, and pepper should all be mixed together in a bowl. Blend well. (4) Press carefully to push the filling into the mushrooms as you stuff them with the quinoa mixture. (5) After preparing a baking dish that is suitable to use in a steam oven, bake the mushrooms for 20 minutes or until they are soft and the tops become golden. (6) As an appetizer or main course, serve warm.

212. Mediterranean Chickpea Salad

Total Time: 20 minutes | Prep Time: 10 minutes

Ingredients:

1 can chickpeas, drained & rinsed	1 cup cherry tomatoes, halved
½ cup cucumber, diced	¼ cup Kalamata olives, sliced
¼ cup red onion, finely chopped	¼ cup crumbled feta cheese
3 tbsp olive oil	1 tbsp red wine vinegar
1 tsp dried oregano	Salt and pepper to taste

Directions:

(1) Salad Ingredients: feta cheese, cucumber, cherry tomatoes, olives, red onion, and chickpeas in a big basin. (2) Combine the oregano, salt, pepper, red wine vinegar, olive

oil, and olives in a shallow basin. Coat the salad evenly by pouring the dressing over it and tossing. (3) Put it in the fridge and eat it right away, or wait up to two hours.

213. Honey Glazed Carrots

Total Time: 25 minutes | Prep Time: 5 minutes

Ingredients:

- 1 lb baby carrots
- 1 tbsp butter
- ½ tsp ground cinnamon (optional)
- 2 tbsp honey
- 1 tsp lemon juice
- Salt and pepper to taste

Directions:

(1) A steam oven should be preheated to 375°F, or 190°C. (2) Transfer the tiny carrots to a pan that can withstand steam. (3) Melt the butter in a small pot. Add the honey, lemon juice, cinnamon (if desired), salt, and pepper. Stir to combine. (4) After mixing the honey and oil, pour it over the carrots and whisk until uniformly coated. (5) After 20 minutes of oven steaming, the carrots should be soft and have a hint of caramelization. (6) As a side dish, serve warm.

214. Thai Peanut Shrimp

Total Time: 30 minutes | Prep Time: 15 minutes

Ingredients:

- 1 lb large shrimp, peeled and deveined
- ¼ cup creamy peanut butter
- 1 tbsp lime juice
- 1 tsp red curry paste
- 2 tbsp chopped peanuts (for garnish)
- ½ cup coconut milk
- 2 tbsp soy sauce
- 1 tbsp brown sugar
- 2 green onions, sliced

Directions:

(1) Heat up the steam oven to a temperature of 375°F, which is equivalent to 190°C. (2) Blend the peanut butter, soy sauce, lime juice, brown sugar, and red curry paste with the coconut milk & soy sauce in a small bowl. (3) Put the shrimp in a steam-safe dish and arrange them in a single layer. After coating the shrimp well, pour the peanut sauce over them. (4) After about a dozen to fifteen minutes of steaming in the oven, the shrimp should be pink and fully cooked. (5) Slice some green onions and cut some peanuts for the garnish. Serve immediately.

215. Pesto Baked Chicken

Total Time: 40 minutes | Prep Time: 10 minutes

Ingredients:

- 4 boneless, skinless chicken breasts
- 1 cup cherry tomatoes, halved
- Salt and pepper to taste
- ½ cup basil pesto (store-bought or homemade)
- ½ cup shredded mozzarella cheese

Directions:

(1) Before using, bring the steam oven up to a temperature of 190°C. (2) Before baking the chicken breasts, season them with salt and pepper. Make sure the baking dish can withstand steam. (3) Apply two teaspoons of pesto to each side of the chicken breasts. Finish with a sprinkling of mozzarella cheese and cherry tomatoes. (4) After 25 to 30 minutes of steaming in the oven, the chicken should be done, and the cheese should be melted and bubbling. (5) Accompany with a dish of fresh salad or steamed veggies and serve hot.

216. Cilantro Lime Rice

Total Time: 25 minutes | Prep Time: 5 minutes

Ingredients:

- 1 cup basmati rice, rinsed
- 1 teaspoon salt
- 1/4 cup fresh cilantro, chopped
- 2 cups water
- 1 lime, juiced and zested

Directions:

(1) Get the steam oven up to a temperature of 100°C (212°F). (2) Mix the water, salt, and washed rice in a pot that can withstand steam. Place a steam-safe lid or foil over the dish to keep it covered. (3) After the water has been absorbed and the rice is soft, transfer the pan to a steam oven and cook for another 18 to 20 minutes. (4) Before mixing in the lime juice, zest, and chopped cilantro, take the rice out of the oven and fluff it with a fork. (5) As a side dish, serve warm.

217. Spaghetti Squash with Garlic Sauce

Total Time: 40 minutes | Prep Time: 10 minutes

Ingredients:

- 1 medium spaghetti squash, halved & seeds removed
- 4 cloves garlic, minced
- 1/4 cup grated Parmesan cheese
- 2 tablespoons olive oil
- 1/4 teaspoon red pepper flakes
- Salt and pepper to taste

Directions:

(1) Get the steam oven up to a temperature of 100°C (212°F). (2) In a steam-safe dish, add a little water and set the spaghetti squash pieces cut side down. Cook until soft, about twenty-five to 30 minutes, in a steamer. (3) Toss the steamed squash into a skillet and heat the olive oil over medium heat. Sauté the garlic and red pepper flakes for one to two minutes or until they begin to smell. Get it out of the oven. (4) Separate the spaghetti squash into strands by scraping it with a fork. Blend in the Parmesan, salt, pepper, and garlic oil. (5) Light enough to eat on its own or as a side dish.

218. Roasted Brussels Sprouts with Bacon

Total Time: 35 minutes | Prep Time: 10 minutes

Ingredients:

- 500g Brussels sprouts, trimmed and halved
- 2 tablespoons olive oil
- 100g bacon, chopped
- Salt and pepper to taste

Directions:

(1) Bring the steam oven up to temperature, preferably using the combined steam setting, which should be 200°C (392°F). (2) Combine the Brussels sprouts, olive oil, salt, and pepper in a baking dish that can withstand steam. Garnish with chopped bacon. (3) Stirring once halfway through roasting, cook sprouts in a steam oven for 25-30 minutes or until edges are caramelized and tender. (4) This savory side dish is best served right away.

219. Baked Ziti with Meatballs

Total Time: 1 hour | Prep Time: 20 minutes

Ingredients:

- 300g ziti pasta
- 2 cups marinara sauce

- 12 small cooked meatballs
- 1 cup shredded mozzarella cheese
- 1 teaspoon dried oregano
- 1 cup ricotta cheese
- 1/4 cup grated Parmesan cheese

Directions:

(1) Get the steam oven up to temperature, using the combined steam setting, if it has one, at 180°C (356°F). (2) To make the ziti al dente, boil salted water and cook for a few minutes. Drain. (3) Arrange the cooked ziti, marinara sauce, meatballs, and ricotta cheese in a casserole dish that can withstand steam. Sprinkle oregano, Parmesan, and mozzarella over the top. (4) Bake for 25 minutes with the foil on top. After 10 more minutes of baking, take the foil off and continue baking until the cheese is melted and brown. (5) Allow to cool for five minutes before consumption.

220. Roasted Chicken and Vegetables

Total Time: 1 hour 15 minutes | Prep Time: 15 minutes

Ingredients:

- 1 whole chicken (1.5kg), patted dry
- 3 tablespoons olive oil
- 1 teaspoon paprika
- Fresh thyme sprigs (optional)
- 500g mixed vegetables (e.g., carrots, potatoes, zucchini), chopped
- 1 teaspoon garlic powder
- Salt and pepper to taste

Directions:

(1) Turn on the steam oven to its combined steam setting and heat it to 200°C (392°F). (2) Chop some garlic powder, sprinkle some salt and pepper on top of the chicken, & then add two teaspoons of olive oil. Preheat a roasting pan & place the items inside. Add salt & pepper to the veggies & toss with the rest of the olive oil. Place the chicken in the center. If preferred, garnish with thyme sprigs. (3) Put the chicken in the steam oven and roast it for an hour, basting halfway through. Make sure it gets to 75°C (165°F) on the inside. (4) Ten minutes should pass before cutting the bird. Top with roasted veggies and serve.

221. Beef Stroganoff

Total Time: 45 minutes | Prep Time: 15 minutes

Ingredients:

- 1 lb beef sirloin, thinly sliced
- 1 medium onion, finely chopped
- 1 cup beef stock
- 2 tbsp Dijon mustard
- 2 tbsp olive oil
- 1 tsp smoked paprika
- 1 cup mushrooms, sliced
- 2 garlic cloves, minced
- 1 cup sour cream
- 2 tbsp flour
- Salt and pepper to taste
- Egg noodles (to serve)

Directions:

(1) A steam oven should be preheated to 375°F, or 190°C. (2) Warm the olive oil in a pan that can withstand steam, and cook the garlic and onions for three minutes. (3) Cook for a further 5 minutes after adding the mushrooms. (4) Flour, smoked paprika, mustard, beef stock, sliced beef, and beef combined. Blend well. (5) After 25 minutes, transfer the dish to the steam oven. (6) Toss in the sour cream, add the salt & pepper, & continue cooking for another five minutes. (7) Top with egg noodles and serve hot.

222. Creamy Pesto Pasta

Total Time: 30 minutes | Prep Time: 10 minutes

Ingredients:

- 12 oz penne pasta
- 1 cup heavy cream
- 1 cup cherry tomatoes, halved
- 1 cup fresh basil pesto
- 1/4 cup grated Parmesan cheese
- 1/4 cup pine nuts (optional, for garnish)
- Salt and pepper to taste

Directions:

(1) Make sure the steam oven is heated up to 350°F (175°C). (2) Toss the pasta with boiling water in a pan that can be used in a steam oven. Cook for 15 minutes, covered. (3) The pesto, heavy cream, and Parmesan cheese should be combined in a different basin. (4) Drain the cooked pasta & combine it with the cherry tomatoes and pesto sauce. (5) For another 5 minutes, heat the pasta mixture in the steam oven until it is well heated. (6) If desired, top with pine nuts before serving.

223. Garlic Parmesan Asparagus

Total Time: 20 minutes | Prep Time: 5 minutes

Ingredients:

- 1 lb asparagus, trimmed
- 2 garlic cloves, minced
- 2 tbsp olive oil
- 1/4 cup grated Parmesan cheese
- Salt and pepper to taste

Directions:

(1) The steam oven should be preheated to 400°F or 200°C. (2) Get a steam-safe platter and lay down the asparagus. Season with salt, pepper, garlic, & olive oil. (3) In a steamer, cook for 12 minutes. (4) After 3 minutes, take the asparagus out of the oven and top it with Parmesan. Bake for a final 3 minutes. (5) For a hot side dish, serve.

224. Cajun Shrimp and Grits

Total Time: 35 minutes | Prep Time: 10 minutes

Ingredients:

- 1 lb large shrimp, peeled and deveined
- 1 cup quick-cooking grits
- 1 cup sharp cheddar cheese, shredded
- 1/4 cup heavy cream
- 1 tbsp Cajun seasoning
- 2 cups chicken stock
- 2 tbsp butter
- 1 tbsp olive oil
- Salt and pepper to taste

Directions:

(1) A steam oven should be preheated to 375°F, or 190°C. (2) Add olive oil and Cajun spice; toss the shrimp. Put them on a tray that can withstand steam and cook them for 8 to 10 minutes in a steam oven. (3) In a skillet that can withstand steam, mix the grits with the chicken stock. Stir midway through the 20 minutes of cooking in the steam oven. (4) After the grits are cooked, combine them with the heavy cream, cheddar cheese, and butter. Finish with a pinch of pepper & salt. (5) Garnish the grits with the Cajun shrimp and serve.

225. Mediterranean Stuffed Eggplant

Total Time: 50 minutes | Prep Time: 15 minutes

Ingredients:

- 2 large eggplants, halved lengthwise
- 1 cup cherry tomatoes, chopped
- 1/4 cup Kalamata olives, chopped
- 2 garlic cloves, minced
- Salt and pepper to taste
- 1 cup cooked quinoa
- 1/2 cup crumbled feta cheese
- 2 tbsp olive oil
- 1 tsp dried oregano

Directions:

(1) A steam oven should be preheated to 375°F, or 190°C. (2) Leave a 1/4-inch margin while scooping out the eggplant flesh. Slice the meat and put it aside. (3) Put the chopped eggplant, cherry tomatoes, garlic, and olives in an oven-safe dish and cook them for 5 minutes in olive oil. (4) Throw in some cooked quinoa, feta, oregano, salt, and pepper, and mix everything together. (5) Put the eggplant halves on a steam-safe dish and stuff them with the mixture. (6) After 35 minutes of steaming, the eggplants should be soft and delicate. (7) Warm it up and top it with fresh parsley if you want.

226. Garlic Parmesan Shrimp

Total Time: 20 minutes | Prep Time: 10 minutes

Ingredients:

- 1 lb (450 g) large shrimp, peeled and deveined
- 1/4 cup grated Parmesan cheese
- 2 tbsp unsalted butter, melted
- 1/4 tsp red pepper flakes (optional)
- Fresh parsley, chopped, for garnish
- 3 garlic cloves, minced
- 2 tbsp olive oil
- 1/2 tsp paprika
- Salt and black pepper, to taste

Directions:

(1) Switch to the steam and bake setting and heat the oven to 175 degrees Celsius. (2) Combine the shrimp, garlic, paprika, olive oil, salt, and pepper in a mixing bowl. (3) On a baking sheet that can withstand steam, evenly distribute the shrimp. (4) Before serving, cover the shrimp with an equal amount of Parmesan cheese & a drizzle of melted butter. To get pink shrimp and golden cheese, steam bake for 8 to 10 minutes. (5) Serve immediately after garnishing with fresh parsley.

227. Stuffed Bell Peppers

Total Time: 45 minutes | Prep Time: 15 minutes

Ingredients:

- Four large bell peppers (any color), tops removed, seeds and membranes scooped out
- Half lb (225 g) ground beef or turkey
- 1/2 cup canned diced tomatoes
- 1 cup cooked quinoa or rice
- 1/2 cup diced onion
- 1/2 cup shredded mozzarella cheese

2 tbsp tomato paste	1 tsp Italian seasoning
Salt and black pepper, to taste	Fresh basil for garnish

Directions:

(1) Put the steam oven on combined heat and bring it up to 375°F, or 190°C. (2) While the pan is heated over medium heat, brown the ground beef. Toss in the chopped tomatoes, onion, tomato paste, salt, pepper, and Italian spice. Bring to a simmer and cook for five minutes. (3) After the rice or quinoa has cooked, add it and stir to combine. (4) After stuffing the bell peppers with the mixture, set them upright in a dish that can withstand steam. (5) 20 to 30 minutes in a steam oven. While cooking for the final 5 minutes, top with mozzarella. (6) Warm the dish before topping it with fresh basil.

228. Coconut Curry Shrimp

Total Time: 30 minutes | Prep Time: 10 minutes

Ingredients:

1 lb (450 g) large shrimp, peeled and deveined	1 tbsp coconut oil
1 small onion, diced	2 garlic cloves, minced
1-inch piece of ginger, grated	1 cup coconut milk
2 tbsp red curry paste	1 tbsp fish sauce
1 tsp sugar	1/2 tsp turmeric powder
Fresh cilantro for garnish	

Directions:

(1) Get the steam oven up to temperature in steam-only mode, which is 350°F or 175°C. (2) Sauté the onion, garlic, and ginger for two to three minutes in coconut oil in a pan that can withstand steam. (3) After 1 minute of stirring, add sugar, turmeric, and curry paste; simmer until aromatic. (4) After adding the fish sauce, whisk in the coconut milk. Lower heat to a low simmer. (5) Sauté the shrimp for 8 to 10 minutes, or until they become pink and are cooked through. (6) Serve over steaming rice and top with cilantro.

229. Lemon Thyme Chicken Thighs

Total Time: 1 hour | Prep Time: 15 minutes

Ingredients:

4 bone-in, skin-on chicken thighs	2 lemons (1 sliced, one juiced)
3 garlic cloves, minced	2 tbsp olive oil
2 tbsp fresh thyme leaves	1 tsp paprika
Salt and black pepper, to taste	

Directions:

(1) Put the steam oven on combined heat and bring it up to 375°F, or 190°C. (2) Combine the garlic, lemon juice, thyme, paprika, olive oil, and pepper as a rub and apply it to the chicken thighs. (3) In a roasting dish that can withstand steam, lay the chicken thighs skin side up. Toss in some lemon wedges and scatter them over the chicken. (4) Bring the chicken to an internal heat of 74°C by steam-baking it for 40-45 minutes. (5) Allow to cool for five minutes before consumption.

230. Honey Glazed Brussels Sprouts

Total Time: 25 minutes | Prep Time: 10 minutes

Ingredients:

1 lb (450 g) Brussels sprouts, halved	2 tbsp olive oil
2 tbsp honey	1 tbsp balsamic vinegar
1/2 tsp garlic powder	Salt and black pepper, to taste

Directions:

(1) In combination mode, bring the steam oven up to 400°F or 200°C. (2) In a mixing dish, combine the Brussels sprouts with the following Ingredients: honey, balsamic vinegar, garlic powder, salt, and pepper. Set aside. (3) Coarsely spread the sprouts out on a baking sheet that can withstand steam. (4) Cook in a steam oven for 18 to 20 minutes, turning once halfway through or until soft and caramelized. (5) As a snack or side dish, serve right away.

231. Thai Basil Beef Stir-Fry

Total Time: 25 minutes | Prep Time: 10 minutes

Ingredients:

1 lb (450g) beef sirloin, thinly sliced	2 tbsp soy sauce
1 tbsp oyster sauce	1 tbsp fish sauce
1 tbsp brown sugar	2 cloves garlic, minced
1 red chili, sliced	1 bell pepper, sliced
1 cup Thai basil leaves	1 tbsp vegetable oil
1 tsp cornstarch mixed with two tbsp water	

Directions:

(1) Start the steam oven at 212 degrees Fahrenheit (100 degrees Celsius). (2) Gather all of the sauce ingredients (cornstarch, soy, oyster, fish, brown sugar) and combine them in a bowl. Ten minutes after adding the steak, let it marinate. (3) In a steam oven-safe dish, combine the garlic, chili, and vegetable oil. Cook on high heat for two minutes. (4) Toss in the peppers and marinated meat, and continue steaming for 8 to 10 minutes more or until done. (5) After the first minute of steaming, add the Thai basil and stir. (6) It goes well with steaming rice.

232. Chicken Fajitas

Total Time: 30 minutes | Prep Time: 10 minutes

Ingredients:

2 boneless, skinless chicken breasts, sliced	1 tsp chili powder
1 tsp cumin	½ tsp smoked paprika
½ tsp garlic powder	Salt and pepper to taste
1 tbsp olive oil	1 red bell pepper, sliced
1 yellow bell pepper, sliced	1 red onion, sliced
Juice of 1 lime	Warm tortillas for serving

Directions:

(1) Start the steam oven at 212 degrees Fahrenheit (100 degrees Celsius). (2) Rub olive oil, cumin, paprika, salt, pepper, and garlic

powder onto the chicken. Marinate it for at least an hour. Chop the onion and peppers and spread them out on a steam-safe plate with the chicken. (3) To ensure the chicken is cooked through, steam it for 12–15 minutes. (4) Pour the juice of the lime over the ingredients. (5) Add warmed tortillas for dipping.

233. Roasted Tomato and Basil Soup

Total Time: 40 minutes | Prep Time: 10 minutes

Ingredients:

6 large tomatoes, halved	1 small onion, chopped
3 cloves garlic, minced	2 tbsp olive oil
Salt and pepper to taste	3 cups vegetable broth
½ cup fresh basil leaves	¼ cup heavy cream (optional)

Directions:

(1) Set the steam oven to convection steam mode and heat it to 400°F or 200°C. (2) Sprinkle salt and pepper over the tomato, onion, and garlic mixture before placing on a baking sheet. Drizzle with olive oil. (3) Cook until tender, about 20 minutes. (4) Puree the roasted veggies in a blender with the vegetable broth. (5) Add the basil leaves, mix, and cook for 10 minutes after pouring into a saucepan. (6) Before serving, heat and stir in heavy cream, if desired.

234. Lemon Garlic Chicken Skewers

Total Time: 35 minutes | Prep Time: 15 minutes

Ingredients:

2 boneless, skinless chicken breasts, cubed	Juice of 1 lemon
2 cloves garlic, minced	1 tbsp olive oil
1 tsp dried oregano	½ tsp salt
½ tsp black pepper	6 wooden skewers (soaked in water)

Directions:

(1) Set the steam oven to convection steam mode and heat it to 375°F, or 190°C. (2) Toss together the oregano, garlic, lemon juice, olive oil, salt, and pepper in a bowl. After 15 minutes of marinating, add the cubes of chicken. (3) Before placing the chicken on a roasting tray, thread it onto skewers. (4) After 15 to 18 minutes of steaming, the meat should be browned and cooked through. (5) Accompany with a side salad or tzatziki sauce.

235. Spicy Roasted Chickpeas

Total Time: 30 minutes | Prep Time: 5 minutes

Ingredients:

1 can chickpeas, drained & rinsed	1 tbsp olive oil
1 tsp smoked paprika	½ tsp cayenne pepper
½ tsp garlic powder	½ tsp salt

Directions:

(1) Turn the convection steam oven up to 400 degrees Fahrenheit (200 degrees Celsius). (2) After drying the chickpeas with a paper towel, put them out on a baking sheet. (3) Paprika, cayenne, garlic powder, salt, and olive oil should be drizzled over the top. (4) Cook, stirring the dish halfway through, for twenty to twenty-five minutes or until golden & crisp. (5)

As a crunchy snack, let it cool a little before eating.

236. Lemon Herb Roasted Chicken Thighs

Total Time: 40 minutes | Prep Time: 10 minutes

Ingredients:

- 4 bone-in, skin-on chicken thighs
- 2 cloves garlic, minced
- 2 tbsp fresh lemon juice
- 1 tsp dried thyme
- Salt and black pepper to taste
- 2 tbsp olive oil
- 1 tbsp lemon zest
- 1 tsp dried oregano
- ½ tsp paprika
- ½ cup chicken broth

Directions:

(1) The steam oven should be preheated to 375°F, or 190°C, with the combination steam mode set to 50% steam and 50% convection. (2) Combine garlic, lemon zest, lemon juice, oregano, thyme, paprika, salt, & pepper in a small bowl. Add the olive oil & stir to combine. (3) Coat the chicken thighs equally with the mixture. (4) Arrange the chicken breast side up in a small baking dish. Cover the chicken with chicken broth. (5) After 30 minutes of roasting, the meat should be 165 degrees Fahrenheit (74 degrees Celsius) inside and have a golden brown color on top. (6) Allow to cool for five minutes before consumption.

237. Creamy Broccoli Soup

Total Time: 30 minutes | Prep Time: 10 minutes

Ingredients:

- 4 cups broccoli florets
- 1 small onion, chopped
- 2 cloves garlic, minced
- One cup heavy cream (or coconut milk for dairy-free)
- ½ tsp black pepper
- 2 cups vegetable broth
- ½ tsp salt
- ½ tsp nutmeg (optional)

Directions:

(1) Turn the steam oven on high heat and get it up to 212 degrees Fahrenheit (100 degrees Celsius). (2) In a dish that can withstand steam, combine the broccoli, onion, and garlic. Permit to steam for fifteen minutes or until soft. (3) Combine with the veggie broth and puree in a blender. (4) Put the ingredients into a saucepan and season with pepper, salt, nutmeg, and cream. To warm thoroughly, cook over medium heat. (5) Top with melted cheese and warm toast.

238. Roasted Sweet Potatoes with Cilantro Lime

Total Time: 35 minutes | Prep Time: 10 minutes

Ingredients:

- 2 large sweet potatoes, peeled and diced
- 1 tsp ground cumin
- Salt and black pepper to taste
- Juice of 1 lime
- 2 tbsp olive oil
- ½ tsp smoked paprika
- 2 tbsp chopped fresh cilantro

Directions:

(1) Turn the steam oven's combined steam setting to 400°F (200°C), which is 30% steam and 70% convection. (2) Combine garlic,

cumin, paprika, olive oil, salt, and pepper with the chopped sweet potatoes. (3) Pour the batter onto a baking pan in an even layer. Cook, stirring once, for 25 minutes. (4) Take it out of the oven, mix with the cilantro & lime juice, & serve hot.

239. Sweet and Sour Pork

Total Time: 40 minutes | Prep Time: 15 minutes

Ingredients:

One lb pork tenderloin, cut into bite-sized pieces	1 tbsp soy sauce
1 tbsp cornstarch	1 tbsp vegetable oil
1 red bell pepper, diced	1 green bell pepper, diced
1 small onion, sliced	1 cup pineapple chunks
For the Sauce:	¼ cup rice vinegar
3 tbsp ketchup	2 tbsp brown sugar
1 tbsp soy sauce	1 tsp cornstarch mixed with two tbsp water

Directions:

(1) Start the steam oven at 375°F, or 190°C, with the combined steam setting set to 40% steam and 60% convection. (2) Combine the meat with the cornstarch and soy sauce. Give it a good ten minutes to marinate. (3) After browning the pork for three minutes in a pan over medium heat, move it to a baking dish. Toss in some pineapple, bell peppers, and onion. (4) Combine the cornstarch mixture, vinegar, ketchup, brown sugar, and soy sauce in a dish & whisk to combine. Top with pork. (5) Twenty minutes of steam-roasting, turning once is all it takes. Heat and serve immediately.

240. Roasted Cauliflower and Spinach Salad

Total Time: 25 minutes | Prep Time: 10 minutes

Ingredients:

1 small head cauliflower, cut into florets	2 tbsp olive oil
½ tsp garlic powder	½ tsp smoked paprika
Salt and black pepper to taste	2 cups fresh spinach
¼ cup toasted almonds	¼ cup crumbled feta cheese (optional)
1 tbsp lemon juice	

Directions:

(1) Turn on the steam oven to a preheated temperature of 200°C, and set it to combination steam or 70% convection. (2) With the help of olive oil, garlic powder, paprika, salt, and pepper, toss the cauliflower. Distribute it onto a baking sheet. (3) Turn once throughout the 15-minute roasting time to ensure even browning. (4) Take it out of the oven and lay it down to cool for a while. (5) Combine spinach, peanuts, feta, and lemon juice; toss to combine. It may be served hot or chilled.

241. Mediterranean Chickpea and Feta Salad

Total Time: 15 minutes | Prep Time: 15 minutes

Ingredients:

1 can chickpeas, drained & rinsed	1 cup cherry tomatoes, halved

½ cup cucumber, diced	¼ cup red onion, finely chopped
¼ cup Kalamata olives, sliced	½ cup feta cheese, crumbled
2 tbsp olive oil	1 tbsp lemon juice
1 tsp dried oregano	Salt and pepper, to taste

Directions:

(1) Warm the chickpeas for 5 minutes in a steam oven set to steam-only mode at 212°F (100°C). (2) Cherry tomatoes, cucumber, red onion, and olives should all be mixed together in a big basin. (3) Serve with refried chickpeas and feta crumbles. (4) After that, add some lemon juice and olive oil, & then season with salt, pepper, & oregano. (5) Combine well and serve right away.

242. Roasted Sweet Potato and Kale Salad

Total Time: 35 minutes | Prep Time: 10 minutes | Cook Time: 25 minutes

Ingredients:

2 medium sweet potatoes, peeled and cubed	2 tbsp olive oil
1 tsp smoked paprika	Salt and pepper, to taste
3 cups kale, chopped	¼ cup dried cranberries
¼ cup walnuts, chopped	2 tbsp balsamic vinegar

Directions:

(1) Turn the steam oven's combined steam setting to 50% steam and heat it to 375°F, or 190°C. (2) Combine sweet potatoes with smoked paprika, olive oil, salt, and pepper. Toss to coat. Transfer to a steam oven baking sheet. (3) Cook, stirring once, for 20 to 25 minutes. (4) Get the kale ready to roast while the sweet potatoes are in the oven. For 2 minutes, steam at 212°F, or 100°C, to soften. (5) Bowl together kale, sweet potatoes that have been roasted, cranberries, and walnuts. Serve by tossing with balsamic vinegar.

243. Lemon Dill Roasted Vegetables

Total Time: 30 minutes | Prep Time: 10 minutes | Cook Time: 20 minutes

Ingredients:

1 zucchini, sliced	1 yellow squash, sliced
1 red bell pepper, diced	1 cup cherry tomatoes, halved
2 tbsp olive oil	1 tbsp fresh lemon juice
1 tsp dried dill	Salt and pepper, to taste

Directions:

(1) Turn the steam oven's combined steam setting to 40% steam and heat it to 400°F (200°C). (2) With the olive oil, lemon juice, dill, salt, & pepper in a dish, combine all of the veggies. Transfer to a steam oven baking sheet. (3) To get a somewhat caramelized and soft texture, roast for twenty minutes, stirring once halfway through. (4) To round off a meal, serve warm as an accompaniment to cereals or on its own.

244. Spinach and Artichoke Stuffed Chicken

Total Time: 40 minutes | Prep Time: 15 minutes | Cook Time: 25 minutes

Ingredients:

- 2 large boneless, skinless chicken breasts
- ½ cup canned artichoke hearts, chopped
- ¼ cup shredded mozzarella cheese
- 1 tbsp olive oil
- ½ tsp black pepper
- ½ cup cooked spinach, chopped
- ¼ cup cream cheese softened
- 1 clove garlic, minced
- ½ tsp salt

Directions:

(1) Turn the steam oven's combined steam setting to 50% steam and heat it to 375°F, or 190°C. (2) Instead of slicing through the chicken breasts, cut a pocket into them. (3) Combine artichokes, garlic, spinach, cream cheese, and mozzarella in a bowl. (4) Put the filling into the chicken breasts and use toothpicks to keep them in place. (5) Add salt & pepper & then drizzle with olive oil. (6) The chicken should reach an internal heat of 74°C after 25 minutes in the oven. (7) After serving, take the toothpicks out.

245. Garlic Herb Roasted Potatoes

Total Time: 35 minutes | Prep Time: 10 minutes | Cook Time: 25 minutes

Ingredients:

- 1 lb baby potatoes, halved
- 2 cloves garlic, minced
- 1 tsp dried thyme
- ½ tsp black pepper
- 2 tbsp olive oil
- 1 tsp dried rosemary
- ½ tsp salt

Directions:

(1) Turn on the steam oven to combined steam mode and heat it to 400°F (200°C). Use 50% steam. (2) Season the potatoes with salt, pepper, rosemary, garlic, and olive oil. (3) Coat a steam oven baking sheet equally. (4) Cook, stirring once, for 25 minutes or until crisp and brown. (5) Garnish with fresh herbs and serve warm.

246. Mediterranean Stuffed Mushrooms

Total Time: 30 minutes | Prep Time: 15 minutes

Ingredients:

- 12 large button mushrooms, stems removed
- 1/4 cup sun-dried tomatoes, finely chopped
- 1/4 cup of coarsely chopped red bell pepper
- 1 clove garlic, minced
- 1/2 teaspoon dried oregano
- 1/2 cup crumbled feta cheese
- 1/4 cup black olives, finely chopped
- 1 tablespoon fresh parsley, chopped
- 1 tablespoon olive oil
- Salt and black pepper to taste

Directions:

(1) Set the steam oven to a temperature of 200°F, or 93°C, using the combined steam and convection setting. (2) In a dish, combine the crumbled mushroom stems with sun-dried tomatoes, olives, bell pepper, parsley, garlic, olive oil, oregano, salt, and black pepper. Add the finely chopped mushroom stems. (3) Pack the filling into the mushroom caps to the brim. (4) In a steam oven with a perforated tray, spread the filled mushrooms out. (5) After 15 minutes of steam baking, the mushrooms should be soft, and the filling should be heated. (6) Warm it up and serve it as a side dish or appetizer.

247. Mediterranean Roasted Vegetables

Total Time: 35 minutes | Prep Time: 10 minutes

Ingredients:

- 1 zucchini, sliced
- 1 eggplant, diced
- 1 red bell pepper, sliced
- 1 yellow bell pepper, sliced
- 1 red onion, sliced
- 1/2 cup cherry tomatoes
- 2 tablespoons olive oil
- 1 teaspoon dried oregano
- 1 teaspoon dried basil
- 1/2 teaspoon garlic powder
- Salt and black pepper to taste

Directions:

(1) Set the steam oven to combination mode (steam and convection) and heat it to 375°F, or 190°C. (2) Combine the veggies in a big basin and add the olive oil, oregano, basil, garlic powder, salt, and pepper. Mix well. (3) Arrange the veggies in a uniform layer on a baking sheet. (4) Stir occasionally while steam-roasting for 25 minutes. (5) Garnish with chopped parsley & serve warm as an accompaniment or topper for salads, pasta, or grain bowls.

248. Stuffed Acorn Squash

Total Time: 50 minutes | Prep Time: 15 minutes

Ingredients:

- 2 acorn squash, halved and seeds removed
- 1/2 pound ground turkey or plant-based alternative
- 1/2 cup quinoa, cooked
- 1/4 cup dried cranberries
- 1/4 cup chopped pecans
- 1 small apple, diced
- 1/2 teaspoon ground cinnamon
- 1/4 teaspoon nutmeg
- Salt and black pepper to taste
- 1 tablespoon olive oil

Directions:

(1) Put the steam oven on combined heat and bring it up to 375°F, or 190°C. (2) Add salt & pepper to the insides of the acorn squash halves after brushing them with olive oil. Cook for 15 minutes with the cut side up on a steam tray with holes in it. (3) Season with salt & pepper, brown the turkey in a skillet, and then combine it with cooked quinoa, cranberries, pecans, apple, cinnamon, and nutmeg. (4) Divide the stuffing mixture among the two halves of the squash. (5) After 20 minutes of baking in the steam oven, the squash should be soft, and the filling should be hot. (6) Keep heated before serving.

249. Creamy Garlic Parmesan Pasta

Total Time: 25 minutes | Prep Time: 10 minutes

Ingredients:

- 8 ounces of fettuccine or pasta of choice
- 2 tablespoons butter
- 3 cloves garlic, minced
- 1 cup heavy cream
- 1/2 cup grated Parmesan cheese
- 1/2 teaspoon salt
- 1/4 teaspoon black pepper
- 1/4 teaspoon red pepper flakes (optional)

1/4 cup chopped fresh parsley

Directions:

(1) Ready the steam oven for use by setting it to full steam at 210°F, or 99°C. (2) Add enough water to a steam-safe dish to cover the pasta. Saute for 8 to 10 minutes, or until crisp-tender, and then remove. (3) While the pan is on medium heat, melt the butter. Sauté the garlic until it releases its aroma. (4) Simmer the heavy cream for two minutes after adding it. (5) Before serving, toss in the Parmesan, salt, pepper, and red pepper flakes (if used). (6) Coat the cooked pasta with the sauce by adding it and tossing. (7) Serve heated with a sprinkle of fresh parsley for garnish.

250. Baked Apple Cinnamon Oatmeal

Total Time: 35 minutes | Prep Time: 10 minutes

Ingredients:

2 cups rolled oats	1 1/2 cups milk or plant-based alternative
1/2 cup unsweetened applesauce	1/4 cup maple syrup or honey
1 teaspoon vanilla extract	1 teaspoon ground cinnamon
1/2 teaspoon nutmeg	1 teaspoon baking powder
1/2 teaspoon salt	1 apple, diced
1/4 cup chopped walnuts or pecans	

Directions:

(1) In combination mode, bring the steam oven up to 350°F, or 175°C. (2) Oats, milk, applesauce, maple syrup, vanilla, cinnamon, nutmeg, baking soda, and salt should all be combined in a dish. (3) Add the chopped apples and almonds. (4) Place the batter in a baking dish that can withstand steam and oil it. (5) Set aside to cool for 25 minutes. (6) Top with yogurt, fresh fruit, or more maple syrup, and serve warm.

251. Honey Mustard Glazed Chicken

Total Time: 40 minutes | Prep Time: 10 minutes

Ingredients:

4 boneless, skinless chicken breasts	¼ cup honey
2 tbsp Dijon mustard	1 tbsp whole-grain mustard
1 tbsp olive oil	1 tsp garlic powder
½ tsp salt	¼ tsp black pepper
Fresh thyme for garnish (optional)	

Directions:

(1) A combined steam oven, using 50% steam and 50% convection, should be preheated to 350°F (175°C). (2) Beets, whole grain mustard, honey, olive oil, garlic powder, salt, and pepper should all be whisked together in a bowl. (3) Brush the honey mustard mixture liberally over the chicken breasts before placing them in a baking tray. (4) Bake, basting halfway through, for 30 minutes in the steam oven. (5) Find out whether the temperature inside is 165 degrees Fahrenheit (75 degrees Celsius). (6) Allow to cool for five minutes before consumption. Top with a sprig of fresh thyme.

252. Maple Glazed Carrots

Total Time: 25 minutes | Prep Time: 5 minutes

Ingredients:

1 lb (450g) baby carrots

1 tbsp olive oil or melted butter

½ tsp salt

2 tbsp maple syrup

½ tsp cinnamon (optional)

¼ tsp black pepper

Directions:

(1) Ready the steam oven for use by setting it to pure steam at 210°F or 100°C. (2) Arrange the carrots in a pan that can withstand steam. (3) Combine the maple syrup, cinnamon, salt, pepper, olive oil (or butter), and a small bowl. (4) Dip the carrots into the glaze & toss them to coat. Leave for 15 minutes to steam until soft. (5) Warm the dish before serving; fresh parsley is an optional garnish.

253. Lemon Herb Baked Chicken Wings

Total Time: 40 minutes | Prep Time: 10 minutes

Ingredients:

2 lbs (900g) chicken wings

1 tbsp lemon juice

2 cloves garlic, minced

1 tsp dried thyme

¼ tsp black pepper

2 tbsp olive oil

1 tsp lemon zest

1 tsp dried oregano

½ tsp salt

Directions:

(1) A combination steam oven, set at 375°F (190°C), with 40% steam and 60% convection, should be preheated. (2) Toss together the olive oil, zest, lemon juice, garlic, oregano, thyme, salt, and pepper on a platter. (3) Marinate the wings for 10 minutes after tossing them in the sauce. (4) Spread the wings out evenly on a baking sheet. (5) Roast for half an hour, turning once. (6) Complement with a slice of lemon and serve when hot.

254. Thai Red Curry Chicken

Total Time: 35 minutes | Prep Time: 10 minutes

Ingredients:

2 boneless, skinless chicken breasts, sliced

2 tbsp Thai red curry paste

1 tbsp brown sugar

1 cup snap peas

1 tsp fresh ginger, grated

1 tbsp lime juice

1 can (13.5 oz) coconut milk

1 tbsp fish sauce

1 red bell pepper, sliced

½ cup bamboo shoots (optional)

1 clove garlic, minced

Fresh basil for garnish

Directions:

(1) Start the steam oven on pure steam mode and heat it up to 210°F, or 100°C. (2) Mix the curry paste, coconut milk, fish sauce, brown sugar, ginger, and garlic in a dish that can be heated in the steamer. (3) Chop some chicken and throw it in with some bell peppers, snap peas, and bamboo shoots. Mix thoroughly. (4) Stir once halfway through the 25-minute steaming period. (5) After taking it out of the oven, mix in the lime juice and top with the fresh basil. (6) Top with steaming rice and serve.

255. Beef and Vegetable Stir-Fry

Total Time: 30 minutes | Prep Time: 10 minutes

Ingredients:

- ½ lb (225g) flank steak, thinly sliced
- 1 tsp cornstarch
- 1 red bell pepper, sliced
- 1 small carrot, julienned
- 2 cloves garlic, minced
- 1 tbsp oyster sauce
- 1 tsp sesame seeds (for garnish)
- 1 tbsp soy sauce
- 1 tbsp sesame oil
- 1 cup broccoli florets
- ½ cup snap peas
- 1 tsp fresh ginger, minced
- 1 tbsp hoisin sauce

Directions:

(1) Set the steam oven to 250°F, which is 120°C, and turn it on. (2) Combine the cornstarch & soy sauce, then add the cut meat. Keep aside for five minutes. (3) Place the steak in a dish that can withstand steam and cook it for 10 minutes. (4) Toss the bell pepper, broccoli, carrots, and snap peas into a separate bowl and steam them for 7 minutes. (5) Before adding the steamed meat and veggies, heat the sesame oil in a skillet and sauté the garlic and ginger. (6) Coat equally with hoisin and oyster sauce by swirling. Simmer for another minute. (7) Hot, garnished with sesame seeds.

256. Thai Basil Beef and Vegetables

Total Time: 25 minutes | Prep Time: 10 minutes

Ingredients:

- 1 lb (450g) beef sirloin, thinly sliced
- 1 small onion, sliced
- 2 cups mixed bell peppers, julienned
- 3 cloves garlic, minced
- 1-inch piece ginger, minced
- 1 tbsp oyster sauce
- 1 tsp brown sugar
- ½ tsp chili flakes (optional)
- 1 tbsp sesame oil
- 2 tbsp soy sauce
- 1 tsp fish sauce
- 1 tsp cornstarch (optional for thickening)
- 1 cup Thai basil leaves

Directions:

(1) Bring the steam oven up to a temperature of 210°F, or 100°C, using medium steam. (2) The soy sauce, oyster sauce, fish sauce, brown sugar, and cornstarch should be combined in a basin. After 5 minutes of marinating, add the cut meat. (3) In a steam-safe dish, combine the meat, garlic, ginger, and onions. Boil for 8 minutes. (4) Before adding the bell peppers and basil, steam for another four minutes. (5) Serve with a drizzle of sesame oil. Hot, served over steaming noodles or rice.

257. Greek Chicken Souvlaki

Total Time: 35 minutes | Prep Time: 15 minutes

Ingredients:

- One lb boneless chicken breast, cut into cubes
- 1 tbsp lemon juice
- 1 tsp dried oregano
- ½ tsp salt
- 2 tbsp olive oil
- 2 cloves garlic, minced
- ½ tsp ground cumin
- ¼ tsp black pepper

Directions:

(1) Combine citrus juice, garlic, cumin, oregano, olive oil, and pepper in a bowl. (2) Rinse the chicken cubes well and set aside for

10 minutes to marinate. (3) Steam the oven until it reaches a temperature of 200°F or 93°C. (4) Skewer the chicken pieces midway through cooking time & place them in a steamer basket with holes. Cook for 15 minutes, flipping once. Top with tzatziki and heated pita bread before serving.

258. Tomato and Mozzarella Salad

Total Time: 10 minutes | Prep Time: 10 minutes

Ingredients:

3 large ripe tomatoes, sliced	8 oz (225g) fresh mozzarella, sliced
1 tbsp balsamic vinegar	2 tbsp extra virgin olive oil
½ tsp salt	¼ tsp black pepper
¼ cup fresh basil leaves	

Directions:

(1) On a platter, alternating the layers of tomato and mozzarella. (2) Toss in some balsamic vinegar & olive oil. Season with pepper and salt. (3) Toss in some fresh basil leaves for garnish. Quickly prepare and serve.

259. Shrimp and Asparagus Stir-Fry

Total Time: 20 minutes | Prep Time: 10 minutes

Ingredients:

1 lb (450g) shrimp, peeled and deveined	1 bunch asparagus, trimmed & cut into 2-inch pieces
3 cloves garlic, minced	1 tbsp soy sauce
1 tbsp oyster sauce	½ tsp sesame oil
½ tsp red pepper flakes (optional)	

Directions:

(1) Get the steam oven up to temperature, then turn the steam on full blast. (2) In a steamer basket, combine the shrimp, asparagus, and garlic. (3) Before the shrimp become pink, steam them for 6 minutes. (4) Mix in the sesame oil, oyster sauce, and soy sauce. (5) Garnish with hot jasmine rice and serve right away.

260. Balsamic Roasted Mushrooms

Total Time: 30 minutes | Prep Time: 10 minutes

Ingredients:

1 lb (450g) button or cremini mushrooms, halved	2 tbsp balsamic vinegar
1 tbsp olive oil	2 cloves garlic, minced
1 tsp dried thyme	½ tsp salt
¼ tsp black pepper	

Directions:

(1) Bring the convection steam to a temperature of 375°F, or 190°C, in the steam oven. (2) Add the garlic, thyme, salt, pepper, balsamic vinegar, and olive oil to the mushrooms. Toss lightly. (3) After that, lay them out evenly on a baking sheet. Turn the roaster halfway through the 20-minute cooking time. (4) This recipe goes well with toasted bread or as a side.

261. Lemon Thyme Roasted Chicken

Total Time: 1 hour 15 minutes | Prep Time: 15 minutes

Ingredients:

1 whole chicken (4-5 lbs)	2 tbsp olive oil
2 tbsp fresh thyme leaves	1 lemon, sliced
4 garlic cloves, minced	1 tsp salt
½ tsp black pepper	½ cup chicken broth

Directions:

(1) Turn the steam oven's combined steam setting to 50% steam and heat it to 375°F, or 190°C. (2) Before seasoning the chicken with salt, pepper, garlic, & thyme, coat it with olive oil. Pat it dry. (3) Fill the cavity with slices of lemon. (4) Spread out a steam-safe baking sheet and set the chicken on top. Add chicken stock to the baking dish. (5) Cook, basting periodically, for 60 to 70 minutes. Turn the chicken over when the thermometer reads 165 degrees Fahrenheit (74 degrees Celsius). (6) Give it 10 minutes to rest before you carve it. Top with pan juices and serve.

262. Lemon Garlic Chicken and Vegetables

Total Time: 40 minutes | Prep Time: 10 minutes

Ingredients:

4 boneless, skinless chicken breasts	1 zucchini, sliced
1 red bell pepper, sliced	1 yellow bell pepper, sliced
2 tbsp olive oil	3 garlic cloves, minced
Juice of 1 lemon	1 tsp dried oregano
½ tsp salt	½ tsp black pepper

Directions:

(1) Turn the steam oven's combined steam setting to 60% steam and heat it to 350°F (175°C). (2) Combine the garlic, lemon juice, oregano, olive oil, salt, and pepper in a bowl. (3) Combine the marinade with the chicken and veggies, then transfer to a steam-safe baking dish. (4) Roast the chicken in a steam oven for 30 minutes or up till the internal heat reaches 74°C. (5) Top with more lemon wedges and serve right away.

263. Thai Red Curry Vegetables

Total Time: 35 minutes | Prep Time: 10 minutes

Ingredients:

1 cup coconut milk	2 tbsp Thai red curry paste
1 zucchini, sliced	1 bell pepper, sliced
1 cup broccoli florets	1 cup snow peas
½ cup baby corn	1 tbsp soy sauce
1 tsp brown sugar	1 tbsp lime juice

Directions:

(1) Turn the steam oven on to 210 degrees Fahrenheit (100 degrees Celsius). (2) Combine the red curry paste, coconut milk, soy sauce, brown sugar, & lime juice in a dish that can withstand steam. (3) Coat the veggies by adding them and tossing them. (4) Cook, stirring once halfway through, for 20 to 25 minutes in a steamer. (5) Naan or steamed jasmine rice would be a good accompaniment.

264. Mediterranean Chicken Skewers

Total Time: 35 minutes | Prep Time: 15 minutes

Ingredients:

Ingredients:

2 boneless, skinless chicken breasts, cubed	1 zucchini, sliced into rounds
1 red bell pepper, cubed	1 yellow bell pepper, cubed
2 tbsp olive oil	1 tsp dried oregano
1 tsp garlic powder	½ tsp salt
½ tsp black pepper	Sticks made of wood that have been immersed in water for half an hour

Directions:

(1) The gas oven should be preheated to 375°F, or 190°C, with 50% steam. (2) Combine the oregano, garlic powder, olive oil, salt, and pepper in a bowl. (3) Skewer the chicken and veggies, then spray them with the marinade. (4) Skewers should be cooked for 20 minutes, with a turn halfway through, on a steam tray with holes in it. (5) Accompany with pita bread and tzatziki sauce.

265. Greek Stuffed Tomatoes

Total Time: 50 minutes | Prep Time: 15 minutes

Ingredients:

4 large tomatoes	1 cup cooked quinoa
½ cup feta cheese, crumbled	¼ cup kalamata olives, chopped
¼ cup red onion, finely diced	2 tbsp fresh parsley, chopped
1 tbsp olive oil	½ tsp dried oregano
Salt and pepper to taste	

Directions:

(1) Turn the steam oven's combined steam setting to 40% steam and heat it to 350°F (175°C). (2) To remove the pulp from tomatoes, cut off the tops. (3) A bowl is the perfect place to mix together quinoa, feta, olives, red onion, parsley, olive oil, oregano, salt, and pepper. (4) Put the tomato halves in a steam-safe dish after stuffing them with the mixture. (5) The tomatoes should be soft when cooked for 30–35 minutes in a steam oven. (6) Warm the dish and top it over with a little olive oil.

266. Balsamic Roasted Garlic Brussels Sprouts

Total Time: 30 minutes | Prep Time: 10 minutes | Cook Time: 20 minutes

Ingredients:

1 lb Brussels sprouts, trimmed and halved	4 cloves garlic, minced
2 tbsp olive oil	2 tbsp balsamic vinegar
1 tsp honey (optional)	½ tsp salt
½ tsp black pepper	

Directions:

(1) Turn the convection steam oven up to 400 degrees Fahrenheit (200 degrees Celsius). (2) Toss the Brussels sprouts in a big basin with the garlic, balsamic vinegar, honey (if desired), salt, and pepper. (3) Using a steam oven tray, evenly distribute the Brussels sprouts. (4) To get a caramelized and tender finish, roast for 18 to 20 minutes, tossing the tray halfway through. (5) Warm it up and put it on the side.

267. Balsamic Chicken Thighs

Total Time: 45 minutes | Prep Time: 10 minutes | Cook Time: 35 minutes

Ingredients:

4 bone-in, skin-on chicken thighs	2 tbsp balsamic vinegar
1 tbsp olive oil	2 cloves garlic, minced
1 tsp Dijon mustard	1 tsp dried oregano
½ tsp salt	½ tsp black pepper

Directions:

(1) Start the steam oven's convection heating system at 375°F, or 190°C. (2) Merge the balsamic vinegar, olive oil, garlic, mustard, oregano, salt, & pepper in a mixing bowl. (3) Marinate the chicken thighs for 5 to 10 minutes by rubbing them with the marinade. (4) The skin side up should be facing the baking dish with the chicken thighs. (5) Cook until browned and done, about 30 to 35 minutes, basting halfway through with pan juices. (6) Pile on top of hot rice or steaming veggies.

268. Spiced Lamb Chops

Total Time: 30 minutes | Prep Time: 10 minutes | Cook Time: 20 minutes

Ingredients:

4 lamb chops	1 tbsp olive oil
1 tsp ground cumin	1 tsp smoked paprika
½ tsp ground coriander	½ tsp salt
½ tsp black pepper	2 cloves garlic, minced
1 tbsp lemon juice	

Directions:

(1) Switch to convection steam mode and heat the steam oven to 400°F or 200°C. (2) Toss together the olive oil, garlic, cumin, paprika, coriander, salt, pepper, and lemon juice on a small platter. (3) Apply the spice blend equally to the lamb chops and set aside for 5 minutes. (4) Put the chops on a steam oven pan & cook for eighteen to twenty minutes, turning once throughout cooking. (5) Top with couscous or roasted veggies and serve warm.

269. Lemon Garlic Shrimp Pasta

Total Time: 25 minutes | Prep Time: 10 minutes | Cook Time: 15 minutes

Ingredients:

8 oz linguine or spaghetti	1 lb large shrimp, peeled and deveined
3 tbsp olive oil	4 cloves garlic, minced
1 tsp red pepper flakes (optional)	Zest and juice of 1 lemon
½ cup cherry tomatoes, halved	¼ cup fresh parsley, chopped
Salt and black pepper to taste	

Directions:

(1) On steam-only mode, bring the steam oven up to 212°F, or 100°C. (2) After 8 to 10 minutes, or until al dente, transfer the pasta to a steam oven pan that has holes punched into it. (3) Prep the garlic and red pepper flakes by sautéing them in olive oil for 1 minute over medium heat in a pan. (4) Before the shrimp become pink, add them to the pan and simmer for another three or four minutes. (5) Add the parsley, cooked pasta, cherry tomatoes, lemon zest, and juice. Mix well. Just a pinch of salt and a little Black Pepper. (6) Instantaneous service is required.

270. Maple Mustard Chicken

Total Time: 40 minutes | Prep Time: 10 minutes | Cook Time: 30 minutes

Ingredients:

- 4 boneless, skinless chicken breasts
- 2 tbsp maple syrup
- 1 tsp apple cider vinegar
- 3 tbsp Dijon mustard
- 1 tbsp olive oil
- ½ tsp salt
- ½ tsp black pepper

Directions:

(1) Start the steam oven's convection heating system at 375°F, or 190°C. (2) Stir together the Dijon mustard, maple syrup, olive oil, vinegar, salt, & pepper in a bowl. (3) Allow the marinade to sit for 5 minutes after coating the chicken breasts with the paste. (4) After twenty-five to thirty minutes of roasting, baste with sauce once. (5) Pair with hot quinoa or steaming green beans for a hearty meal.

THE END

Printed in Great Britain
by Amazon

d3a3b0af-217a-46a8-834c-3b6c1fa8609fR01